HOW TO HYPNOTIZE
(Hetero Hypnosis)

Living With Hypnosis Series

HOW TO HYPNOTIZE

(Hetero Hypnosis)

by

ALBERTO HIDALGO, M.D.

and

JACK I. GRAY, *Psychologist*

BORDEN PUBLISHING COMPANY
2623 San Fernando Road, Los Angeles, California 90065

Printed in the United States of America by—

BORDEN PUBLISHING COMPANY
2623 San Fernando Road, Los Angeles, California 90065

They were told,

      "THERE WILL BE NO PAIN."

AND THERE WAS NONE!
FOR THEY BELIEVED AND IT WAS SO.
THE SCIENCE OF HYPNOSIS
MAKES THIS POSSIBLE

CONTENTS

PREFACE

Surgeries are performed while they talk, sing or dream; teeth are extracted while they watch imaginary movies, and all without anesthesia of any kind. Limbs are made immovable and set in awkward positions to remain for long periods of time without plaster casts. Women bear children without fear or pain, disease is arrested and the aches and soreness from rheumatism, arthritis and the like are alleviated. No longer is there fear or pain in the minds or bodies of those plagued with incurable disease . . . BECAUSE THEY LISTENED AND THEY BELIEVED WHEN THEY WERE TOLD . . . "THERE IS NO PAIN!" . . . AND THERE WAS NONE!!!

The merging of hypnosis with the many professions and vocations, medical and non-medical, shows there is a need for further development of methods and techniques suitable for all purposes. Crucial to the science of hypnosis is that the methods and techniques of hypnotizing be developed as an organized methodology of hypnotic therapy. At present, hypnosis is deprived of its status as a disciplined science. It is used in many ways, and in particular for therapeutic purposes.

Scientific tradition, which considers internal factors, demands more knowledge be attained and evaluated through experience before hypnosis is accepted as a true science.

We have consolidated our knowledge and experience to convey to the reader some facts about hypnosis proving that it can help in the pursuit of health and happiness and to reveal some of the secrets of hypnotizing. The annals of history show a marked degree of secrecy was involved in the way it was taught to others. Less revealing was the manner in which IT WAS APPLIED. Because of this the science of hypnotism of today, must of necessity, start at the very root and foundation from which this science was born. Evidence compels us to lay a new foundation and be careful in how we lay it. Upon this hinges its success.

We are, at present, interested in one phase of this great science, "HOW TO HYPNOTIZE." We are also interested in LIVING WITH HYPNOSIS, to teach it and use it to better man's way of life. We are obligated to the science to do our part to teach the art of LIVING WITH HYPNOSIS scientifically. With the knowledge and understanding of applying it correctly and the manner in which it should be utilized, the science of hypnosis will advance to its proper place among the other sciences.

Experience taught us to believe that the interest in hypnotism leads one to try it sooner or later either as a subject or as an operator. It best be known that in inexperienced hands, hypnosis can be dangerous.

When a subject becomes excited, hysterical or is afraid he will not awaken, or be made to do things against his will, negative reactions may ensue. No person should allow anyone to hypnotize him without having professional support present. The future of this science depends upon those who use it and the responsibility of its being applied properly rests on those who teach it.

Professional hypnotists claim hypnosis can control or govern every part of the human body. We know it can control the mind and the five senses. The internal factors are the organs within the body and how they are effected by suggestions under hypnosis. The suggestions acting as external stimuli effect amnesia, analgesia, anesthesia, illusions, delusions and hallucinations. The internal response is caused by the senses creating the necessary action which controls and governs the effects that are produced. Therefore, it is possible that every part of the anatomy can be controlled through hypnosis.

The significance of being able to control mind and matter opens a new school of thought wherein; a doctor can condition patients before and after surgery to respond in accord with directions, and during the operation to react to what he is told as long as it is for his benefit and welfare. The doctor would then be able to control blood pressure, respiration, temperature, organs, glandular action, etc. The patient can be conditioned to dream while undergoing surgery. To have a calm mind and a contented feeling before, during and after surgery. Pain can be controlled, sedation reduced or eliminated and a suggestion can be applied to the effect that healing and convalescence will be excellent and quick.

The study of hypnosis will provide a better understanding of what it is all about and possibly incite the desire to become one who will champion the science instead of condemning or censuring its use. Those who have justification in using hypnosis have deliberately neglected to take advantage of this means of helping mankind because of the length of time it usually has taken to devote to the induction. Time is important, therefore methods of induction should involve procedures which eliminate needless waste of time. In the series of LIVING WITH HYPNOSIS, techniques which are quick and easy to use will be revealed.

This book contains the basic principals of how to hypnotize, "HETERO HYPNOSIS." It will enlighten your mind on the subject and unfold to you a world of wonders, amazing to behold and yours to live in, yours to take advantage of, or to share with others. You have the choice. To those who will delve further into the wonders of hypnotism we can only say that the rewards will be greater than they expect to find.

Alberto Hidalgo, M.D.

Jack I. Gray, Psychologist

INTRODUCTION

Hypnosis cannot be induced without some form of suggestion present to activate the mind. When a suggestion takes effect it is because it is acting as a stimulus on one or more of the senses, causing the subconscious mind to respond automatically. An example of this being true to form can be found in our daily lives. Our lives are ruled by the power of suggestion either supplied from within our own minds or from another person or thing. Examples: When a lemon is squeezed before our eyes, we automatically taste the juice, but we have not touched the lemon or swallowed any juice. The aroma of our favorite food cooking will also effect us automatically and cause us to have some or desire it.

Each of the senses has the ability to function independently of one another, but we can cause one to act in sympathy with another or direct it, through suggestion, to effect all of them at the same time. The depth of hypnosis depends on the kind of suggestions that are used when hypnotizing a person. It is very important to know the kind of suggestions which induce the condition of hypnosis and what form of suggestions are responsible for the depth attained. It is also necessary to know and understand how to maintain the depth of hypnosis and the control of the individual at all times. It is accomplished by the use of the correct suggestions applied at the proper time.

The prime factors responsible for a deep hypnotic

condition are: 1. SUGGESTIONS CAPABLE OF ACT-ING AS A SEDATIVE TO THE BRAIN AND SENSES, INSTEAD OF A STIMULUS. THE PURPOSE IS TO STILL THE MIND AND CALM THE SENSES FIRST. TO INDUCE DEEP HYPNOSIS, BEFORE ALERT-ING THEM TO PERFORM OR ACT. 2. TESTING FOR DEPTH. TO KNOW THE KIND OF TEST TO USE TO FIND OUT JUST WHERE IN HYPNOSIS AND IN WHAT CONDITION THE HYPNOTIZED PERSON IS IN. 3. WHAT TO DO AND WHAT NOT TO DO IN EACH AND EVERY STAGE AND STATE OF HYPNOSIS. 4. THE ABILITY OF THE HYP-NOTIST TO OBSERVE VISUAL SIGNS OF HYP-NOSIS AT WORK WHEN THEY APPEAR. 5. TO KNOW WHAT TO DO WHEN A SUBJECT GOES INTO HYPNOSIS EITHER TOO SLOW OR TOO FAST.

There are no two minds alike. Each individual will respond to hypnosis in a different manner. It is there-fore, very essential that we depend solely on our own ability as hypnotists to influence the mind to react in accord with suggestions which will bring on the re-sults we desire to achieve.

The proper use of positive suggestions definitely impress the mind through the senses. They may be ap-plied by words, signs, looks or touch. They are re-corded on the subconscious mind and either conscious-ly or unconsciously cause an individual to respond. In hypnosis, we endeavor to control the conditions pro-duced by the suggestions. The kind of suggestions which are especially used in hypnotism are as follows:

DIRECT SUGGESTION . . . Used to communicate

directly with another mind with the possibility of one or more minds being free to receive the suggestion.

SENSORY SUGGESTION . . . Received through the senses: Optical, Auditory, Tactile, Olfactory and Gustatory. (Seeing, Hearing, Touch, Smell and Taste.)

HYPNOTIC SUGGESTION . . . Natural or induced by word, act, look, touch or any other method of communication to the passive mind of a person.

POST HYPNOTIC SUGGESTION . . . Takes effect after the hypnotic session when the individual awakens from the hypnotic sleep. It may take effect immediately or sometime later after the awakening. It depends upon the depth of hypnosis achieved and on the hypnotist's suggestions.

INDIRECT SUGGESTION . . . The introduction or implantation of anything to the conscious mind, by word or act, which has the ability to alert the subconscious mind to respond in some way or manner.

AUTO SUGGESTION . . . Given by the conscious mind to the subconscious mind. It is a valuable aid to self improvement and performs wonders when applied with a firm and steadfast belief in one's self. It is the key that unlocks the door to self hypnotic control. This form of suggestion is responsible, in many ways, for the habitual things in our life. Miraculous cures of sickness and disease, through auto suggestion, have been performed by many people. Witnessed accounts of some of these cures have appeared in national newspapers and magazines. Auto suggestion is the strongest form of suggestion to use in SELF HYPNOSIS

The next book to be issued to the public, from this

series of LIVING WITH HYPNOSIS, will be on HOW TO ATTAIN AND PRACTICE SELF HYPNOSIS. The way to formulate suggestions and the manner in which they should be applied to gain self hypnotic control will be revealed in this book.

Direct suggestions have a tendency to arouse the rebellious nature within us. We do not like to be told what to do. The indirect approach into hypnosis seems to be the better way. Better results in attaining a deeper condition and more control can be gained by using indirect suggestions. We are easily aroused when curiosity gets the best of us and often we dare to venture into things because of our curious nature. As hypnotists, through indirect suggestions, we can arouse an individual's curiosity and hold him spellbound, thus inhibiting the senses, by using the power of suggestion. The influence of hypnosis then begins to work causing the conscious mind to become still and allowing the subconscious to become obedient to suggestions from the hypnotist.

Some of the things to remember when you endeavor to hypnotize a person are:

1. Frequency and repetition of words such as relax, rest, tired, drowsy, sleepy, etc., will bring on a tranquil feeling.

2. Creating lasting impressions on the mind of things well liked and desired will cause a person to respond to hypnotic suggestions.

3. Fixation of attention using objects which are fascinating to watch such as spirals, crystal balls, colored lights, etc., will ease mental tension.

4. Monotonous voice, sounds and noises will calm and soothe the nerves.

5. Limiting the field of awareness will help calm the conscious mind.

6. Limiting the voluntary movements of the limbs will attract the subconscious mind.

7. Inhibiting ideas and associations will also calm the conscious mind and alert the subconscious.

8. Familiar things in a strange place will arouse curiosity and alert the subconscious mind.

9. Abnormal position of anything will direct and increase the attention of the conscious mind and stimulate the subconscious.

10. Abnormal shape of things generally seen in normal shape will attract the conscious mind and hold it's attention because of curiosity, and stimulate the subconscious mind.

How can you tell when a person is responding to hypnotic suggestions? Can you observe hypnosis at work? Are there visual signs which can be seen and detected? Can these stages and states of hypnosis be recognized? These are some of the many questions you will be concerned with. The answers will be forthcoming as you continue to read.

There are definite means of identifying every degree, stage and state of hypnosis. From the very instant hypnosis takes effect there is an immediate disturbance or change of the usual normal functions of the body and limbs, especially in motion and sensation. The changes are caused by objects of fascination in one form or another which effect the senses. The hypnotist's voice becomes an object of fascination as soon as he begins his monotonous way of talking. The skillful hypnotist is able to use almost anything at hand as an object of fascination to attract the attention of the conscious mind. The intension is to influence the physical senses and strengthen the verbal suggestions.

The normal actions of the hands, arms, feet and legs are disturbed by hypnosis and are either stopped or placed in some unusual or awkward position. Hypnosis produces a condition parallel to paralysis on the moving parts of the body such as the eyelids and limbs which are generally in constant motion. You can tell when a person is responding to hypnotic suggestions by observing the common, usual motions of the eyelids and limbs and perceiving the changes as they occur.

When a person is influenced by hypnotic suggestions the immediate effect is on the action of the eyelids. The blinking slows and the eyelids take on the appearance of being heavy and hard to stay open. Sometimes the eyelids cease to move and remain open for a long period of time without blinking. The eyes, usually moving all of the time, become still and stare straight ahead. The eyelids become very heavy, a tired look appears on the face followed by involuntary fluttering of the eyelids and the closing of the eyes. Swallowing almost ceases, slowing of the rhythm of pulse and breath follows. Normal motions of the arms and legs slow up and stop. As physical and mental tension is released, the individual goes deeper and deeper until he is in a special kind of sleep. He is not in the sleep we retire into each night, he is in a condition RESEMBLING SLEEP and is able to respond to suggestions.

Observing the voluntary and involuntary movements

before any attempt to hypnotize is made, will help to recognize the changes as visual signs of hypnosis. They act as a guide and direct you to either deepen the condition of hypnosis or continue to work in the stage or state already attained.

The visual signs are always present . . . Sometimes appearing slowly, easily to detect and at times too fast for the eyes to follow. The more observant and alert you are to the signs, the more successful you will be in the practice of hypnosis.

During deep hypnosis, the subject appears to be asleep. You must always remember that it is only the resemblance to sleep and must, therefore, be able to distinguish the difference between natural sleep and the hypnotic sleep. The visual signs definitely show that hypnosis is present and at work long before the sleep condition appears. In normal sleep, the conscious mind is unconscious and unaware of anything happening in the room. In the hypnotic sleep, the conscious mind is only stilled, calm and is aware of what is going on, but nothing can disturb or bother it in any way as long as there is rapport between it and the hypnotist. In this condition, the senses are alert and susceptible to suggestion.

The amount of control we have of the senses depends on the depth of hypnosis. There are three states of hypnosis. The average person recognizes these as being the LIGHT, MEDIUM and DEEP DEGREES. Scientifically these are classified as the HYPNOIDAL, CATALEPTIC and SOMNAMBULISTIC STATES. These are the true and genuine states of hypnosis. There are two other states of hypnosis called the WAKING STATE and PSEUDO HYPNOSIS.

The waking state is primarily used to test a person to find out how susceptible he is to suggestions before trying to hypnotize him. Pseudo Hypnosis is used in stage and entertainment fields. One of the books to be published in the future in this series of LIVING WITH HYPNOSIS will be entitled PSEUDO HYPNOSIS. It will reveal some of the secrets of stage hypnotists and how they accomplish their amazing feats without using hypnosis.

Before you endeavor to hypnotize anyone you should know the basic principals and general rules of hypnotizing, professionally called Hetero Hypnosis. Our objective is to provide you with the proper kind of knowledge and the means to use it so that you can become an expert hypnotist. There is a growing demand for expert men and women hypnotists. There are many fields to work in, especially medicine, dentistry, hypnotherapy, optometry, etc.

We feel responsible to the reader and express our desire that you read carefully the instructions herein contained. Do not begin to practice before you are well acquainted with the information you find within the pages of this book.

Before we go further, let us consider the word SUBJECT. It is not a good word to use when we refer to the person who is to be hypnotized or is hypnotized. It implies that the individual is being subjected to the will of the hypnotist. We shall not use the word SUBJECT when we are referring to the person who is being hypnotized, we shall instead, use the word HYPNOTEE from now on. in all of the books to be published in this series.

Science is a systemized body of facts ascertained by observation and verification. Hypnotism is now an accepted science. It has been observed, tested and verified by other sciences to be useful to mankind. It has been acclaimed as one of the greatest aids to all of the sciences. The science of hypnotism is on the advance and constantly proving its worth and value to mankind in medicine, dentistry, obstetrics, etc., as well as in all walks of private life.

The need for better understanding and a more unified way of learning about this science has been made by those who seek to learn how to use this science correctly. We endeavor to supply this need by writing this series in a concise and simplified manner for all to understand.

THE WAKING STATE
(Waking Hypnosis)

This state is used to test individuals to find out just how suggestible they are and how fast they will respond to hypnosis. In the past, these tests were applied to all individuals to be hypnotized. Today they are seldom used because too much time is wasted putting a person through all of the tests. The only time a professional hypnotist will use these tests is when he desires to condition a person to accept hypnosis, teaching self hypnosis, or when he is demonstrating stage hypnosis. Every student must learn how to tell the difference between people who are susceptible to hypnosis and those who are not. Using the waking state, the student is able to tell whether or not he will succeed in hypnotizing.

There are many of these tests, when used properly, help to detect the kind of hypnotee the person will be. Here are the five most important tests.

1 . . . . THE HAND CLASP TEST: The advantage of using this test first is to enable the hypnotist to tell quickly whether or not a person can be hypnotized in a short time, quick and easy. If the individual responds well to this test, in all probability, he can be hypnotized quite easily. The tests are used to gain authority, therefore, the voice of the hypnotist must be authoritative. The intention is to establish a firm rapport as quick as possible and perhaps induce hypnosis there and then if the response is good. In testing we use

DIRECT SUGGESTIONS and they are spoken with authority and directive force. The HAND CLASP TEST is performed using the following words:

"Place your hands together interlocking the fingers. Squeeze your hands and fingers together and lock them tight, as tight as you can. Squeeze them hard and lock them tighter together. Feel the hands and fingers locking themselves tight together. Squeeze harder and harder until the color in the fingers and hand change to almost white. Lock them more firmly, squeeze harder and harder until they become stuck together. Tightly stuck, locked together, locked tightly together. Locked tight, stuck fast together. They are tightly locked now and stuck together, stuck fast together and you cannot open them! They are tightly locked! Stuck together so tight they are glued together and you cannot open them! No matter how hard you try, you cannot open them! You cannot open them! You cannot, no matter how hard you try, you cannot open them! Try, try to open them, you cannot! You cannot open them until I tell you that you can! Stop trying and open your hands. Unlock your fingers and relax, relax, relax!"

If the individual is unable to open the hands and take them apart, he is very suggestible and is susceptible to hypnosis. The induction into hypnosis should be started and a test for catalepsy applied immediately. If the entire arm can be made stiff and rigid and the individual cannot move or bend it, he is in the cataleptic state. It can be done in less than five minutes. If the individual takes his hands apart without struggling to loosen them and shows no look of surprise on his face, he will not be quickly and easily hypnotized. If an individual makes no effort to unclasp his hands and a look of surprise appears in any way, (by the expression on the face or nervous action in the hands or fingers, such as trembling, etc.) he is either in deep catalepsy or light somnambulism. He can be told to close his eyes and sleep and he will obey and comply with your suggestions from then on until he is told to awaken. More about the cataleptic and somnambulistic states will be in later chapters.

When a person has not responded to the first test, the second test is immediately applied. If necessary to go through all of the tests, time should not be wasted between testing. Also the intention is to condition the person to accept what you say to be so and to follow your directions without analyzing what is going on.

2 . . . . THE BACKWARD FALLING TEST: Place the individual standing in a position of attention with the hands and arms straight down the side of the body. The heels and toes must be flat on the floor, heels together and toes together. Tilt the head slightly up and back. Direct the person to close his eyes and to look up into the head keeping his eyes upward at all times until you tell him that he can bring them down and open his eyes. Stand behind him with your hands on his shoulders, bearing down slightly so that the weight of your hands rests on his shoulders. Tell him that he is going to fall back into your hands when you tell him to do so and to expel any fears he may have of falling back on to the floor. You want him to try going back so that he can see for himself that he cannot fall down and that no harm can come to him. Impress upon his mind the fact that he cannot fall because you are in

back of him and will catch him. Demonstrate this by pulling him back and catching him at least three times. When you feel he is swaying back without any pressure from your hands, take your hands away from the shoulders and repeat the following words:

"You are falling back, falling back, back, back into my hands. I will catch you. Something is pulling you back. You can feel it. You feel it pulling now and it is causing you to come back. You are falling! Let yourself go. Do not resist the urge to fall back. The more you resist this force which is pulling strongly on your back and shoulders, the harder it is to remain standing still. You feel it pulling and you are letting yourself go back. FALLING! FALLING BACK, BACK, BACK! COMING BACK NOW, FALLING, FALLING, FALLING BACK!"

If the individual begins to fall back quickly and easily, he is amenable to external stimuli. He is very suggestible and can be hypnotized in a short while with the proper suggestions which will apply to the senses directly. As an example: "Your eyes are tired and your eyelids are getting heavy." This type of suggestion is directed to something which he can feel on the outside of his body. His imagination provides the means whereby he responds. Therefore, any suggestion which will tend to arouse the imagination will help to induce hypnosis quickly and easily on this type of person.

If the person does not respond in any way to the suggestions of falling during the test, his imagination cannot be aroused quickly. This type of person responds more readily when his curiosity is aroused. Many times the individual tested will state, "If you had continued a while longer, I would have fallen back." In this case the person had confidence in you and in his own ability to respond properly BUT HE DID NOT FEEL SAFE AND SECURE IN YOUR ABILITY TO CATCH HIM AND KEEP HIM FROM FALLING TO THE FLOOR. The next test will show that this is true. It is simple and easy. It is one that is often used to trick a person into believing that he is hypnotized.

3 . . . . THE EYELID TEST: This is another pseudo hypnotic trick to convince a person you can hypnotize him. We use this trick hypnotic effect to gain more prestige and obedience to our suggestions. We can also tell whether or not the individual is susceptible to indirect suggestions and less authority. It will also expose his willingness to cooperate.

The individual tested is told to keep his eyelids closed and to look up into the head or on the forehead where the hypnotist has placed a finger. It is usually placed in the center of the forehead or on the hairline. The entire procedure takes but a few moments and it should result in a positive response as long as the individual keeps his eyes looking upward. The following words are spoken in a well modulated voice injecting the feeling in the tone of voice that the eyelids are unable to open. The words should have feelings which infer that you are certain that he cannot open them.

"Make yourself as comfortable as you can and relax. Just relax. Close your eyes. I am going to place my finger on your forehead. Look up at the spot where my finger is and keep your eyelids closed. KEEP

THEM CLOSED. GAZE INTENTLY ON THE SPOT MY FINGER IS ON AND DO NOT MOVE YOUR EYES AWAY FROM IT. YOUR EYELIDS ARE HEAVY, VERY HEAVY, TOO HEAVY TO OPEN. DO NOT TRY TO OPEN THEM UNTIL I TELL YOU TO TRY. KEEP YOUR EYES UPWARD UNTIL I TELL YOU TO BRING THEM DOWN. LOOK UP. LOOK UP. LOOK UP. YOUR EYELIDS ARE SO VERY HEAVY NOW, YOU CANNOT OPEN THEM. YOU JUST CANNOT PULL THEM OPEN, NO MATTER HOW HARD YOU TRY. THEY JUST REFUSE TO OBEY YOUR EFFORTS TO OPEN. YOU CANNOT AND WILL NOT BE ABLE TO OPEN THEM. LOOK UP. LOOK UP. LOOK UP. NOW TRY TO OPEN THEM. YOU CAN'T! YOU CANNOT OPEN THEM! STOP TRYING AND OPEN YOUR EYES."

If you have correctly applied the test, the eyelids could not have opened IF THE INDIVIDUAL KEPT HIS EYES LOOKING UPWARD. IT IS PHYSICALLY IMPOSSIBLE TO DO SO. The eyes must come down before the eyelids can be opened. If the response was good the person can be told to keep his eyes closed and relax. When you say relax, he will automatically bring his eyes down and feel tired from the strain of keeping the eyes upward. The induction into hypnosis may be tried at this time.

If the response was negative and the individual appears tired but wide awake and alert, we go into the next test which will help tire him down to become more susceptible to suggestions. We can either use a pendulum, which is known as Cheveroul's Pendulum (a glass ball on a chain) or else we can use the arm levitation test. Have him hold the end of the chain and by suggesting to him that the ball is swinging in a certain direction, have him concentrate on making it move that way. There are many varieties of tests which can be used but most of them take up too much time. Up to date this wasting of time has been one of the chief complaints against the use of hypnosis. We endeavor to eliminate this compaint which has been so detrimental to the science by supplying more efficient and quick ways of inducing hypnosis.

We choose to use the arm levitation test as the most effective of the two mentioned above. It is the intention of the hypnotist to cause an arm to rise without any voluntary action on the part of the person he is trying to hypnotize. In the previous test notice the tone change in the voice. The objective for changing the voice now to a soft and soothing one is to find out whether or not we can talk the individual into responding by arousing his imagination, curiosity, cooperation, willingness and respect for himself as well as to build a firmer belief in himself that he can do it by himself.

4 . . . . THE ARM LEVITATION TEST: Place the individual to be tested in a chair and direct him to make himself as comfortable as he can and listen to the directions you will give him. Place one arm with the elbow, forearm and hands either on the arm of the chair or on the thigh. It should be in a loose and comfortable position. Tell him to gaze on the back of the hand, to concentrate on it heavily. Suggest to him that he will not allow anything to interfere with him as long as you are directing him. Begin to calm your

voice down to a soft soothing tone and repeat the following words:

"You are just relaxing, quietly resting and relaxing. Do not allow anything to bother you or disturb you in any way or manner. Just relax and listen to my voice. Let me guide you. Let me direct you. Just relax and listen. Pay close attention to my voice. You are relaxing very easily now and beginning to feel tired. Concentrate on your hand and watch it slowly rise without any effort on your part whatsoever. It is relaxed and getting lighter. Lighter and lighter with each moment that passes. Just keep on relaxing and watch the back of your hand as it slowly begins to rise as though it is floating in the air. It is so light, getting lighter and lighter now. You can feel it moving, gently, slowly moving. Every nerve and muscle in the entire arm is completely relaxed. You can feel it going up, going up, rising, slowly but surely rising and you cannot hold it down. You do not want to hold it down, it feels so good, so light, so very light. It is going up, up, up, higher and higher, getting lighter and lighter. No longer can you hold it down or resist letting it go. Going up, up, up. Still rising higher and higher. Let it go now faster and easier, still higher. The hand is moving up and toward your face. The moment it touches your chin you will let yourself go into a deep, refreshing sleep. Just for a while, you will let yourself go into sleep. A delightful, soothing sleep. Your arm is still rising higher and higher up toward your chin. Soon it will touch your chin and when it does, your eyelids will close and you will drift away into sleep. (IF THE ARM HAS GONE UP AND DOES TOUCH

THE CHIN, THE INDUCTION INTO DEEPER HYP-
NOSIS SHOULD TAKE PLACE NOW. IF THERE
HAS BEEN A RESPONSE, BUT IT IS NOT QUITE
SATISFACTORY, BECAUSE TOO MUCH TIME IS
BEING TAKEN UP TILL NOW, THE INDIVIDUAL
SHOULD BE TOLD TO RELAX THE ARM COM-
PLETELY AND LET IT BECOME NORMAL AND
NATURAL IN EVERY WAY. HE SHOULD BE TOLD
THAT IT WAS A GOOD TRY AND NEXT TIME HE
WILL DO BETTER).

If the individual has not succeeded in raising the
arm, he should be given the next test. It is the last one
we recommend at this time. This test is also physically
impossible to fail because it is a pseudo hypnotic trick.
It is performed to impress an individual with the
thought that if you really wanted to hypnotize him,
you could do it. It is called the WALL TEST. The intention of the hypnotist is to endeavor to still the conscious mind of the person he wants to hypnotize quick
and fast. This trick will often stop a person from thinking for a few moments, giving the hypnotist time to
instill hypnotic suggestions.

5 . . . . THE WALL TEST: Place the person to be
tested standing against a wall with one foot and one
shoulder touching the wall and the other foot and
shoulder facing the opposite wall. The feet should be
spread apart at least twelve inches. Direct him to stand
straight up and allow all of his weight to bear down
on his feet. Tell him to concentrate on how heavy he
is and think that all of his weight is now concentrated
on the feet. Place your hand or a finger on the top of
the arm very close to the shoulder. Hold it there lightly

and tell him that as long as you have your finger at that spot, he will not be able to raise a leg. His feet will be stuck to the floor and the shoulder to the wall, as long as your finger is on his arm. Talk to him in a commanding tone and look at him with the expression on your face that it is just impossible for him to move a leg until you tell him to do so. Advise him to that effect and go ahead with the following words.

"Stand against the wall with both feet flat on the floor and do not attempt to move a foot until I tell you to do so, for you will not be able to move either foot or leg until I permit you to do so. You cannot move. You cannot raise a foot, no matter how hard you try to do so, you will not be able to raise a foot. TRY! YOU CANNOT! YOU CANNOT! TRY HARD! YOU CANNOT! STOP TRYING! Relax and do as you please."

This test will fail only when a person knows that it is impossible to move a leg or raise a foot while standing in that position with the shoulder touching the wall. If the person knows of this, then have him remove the shoulder but LEAVE THE WRIST TOUCHING THE WALL. THIS WILL ACCOMPLISH THE SAME PURPOSE. There will always be a positive result when using this pseudo hypnotic trick. The individual will usually believe that he was hypnotized and before he has time to think or analyze what has happened, he is told to be seated and relax. The hypnotist should then immediately try to hypnotize him into the first stage of hypnosis, or repeat the following words:

"You are perfectly normal and natural in every way. All of the tiredness, heaviness and drowsiness which may be existing within your body is gone. You feel pleasantly warm and comfortable and are just relaxed. All tension is gone from your body and mind. You have complete control of yourself in every way. You are well able to do as you please from now on."

It is not mandatory to use any or all of the tests on each and every individual you try to hypnotize. But, until you have gained some experience in hypnotizing, it is advisable to test your prospective hypnotees. By doing so you will have less failures and gain more confidence in yourself and in the ability to hypnotize.

Frequently a person will respond to tests fairly well, but will fail to respond to hypnosis. Conversely, one who will be completely negative to the tests will react to efficacious suggestions in a hypnotic patter. REMEMBER TO COUNTERMAND ALL SUGGESTIONS, WHICH ARE NOT IN ANY WAY HELPFUL OR BENEFICIAL TO THE PERSON! YOU ARE RESPONSIBLE FOR HIS WELFARE AND WELL BEING AT ALL TIMES. THEREFORE, ALWAYS COUNTERMAND YOUR SUGGESTIONS OF BEING TIRED, HEAVY, DROWSY, ETC., BEFORE YOU LEAVE THE HYPNOTEE ON HIS OWN RESPONSIBILITY.

Practice will develop your ability to recognize how susceptible to suggestions a person is before you try to hypnotize him. There are many ways and means of developing your power of suggestion and the ability to use it. They are all used in the waking state. As an example: If a person is with you and you are standing talking about things in general, walk to a chair and sit down without saying anything. If he follows and wants to do likewise, suggest to him to sit in a chair other than the one he has chosen. If he responds without saying anything, suggest other things to him which seem trivial, especially insignificant things not in relation to what you are talking about. If he is a smoker, and you are too, take your cigarette out of your pack and don't attempt to light it, see if he will offer you a light. You can also pretend that you are reaching for a cigarette and see if he responds to your suggestion to smoke. There are numerous ways of testing a person to find out how susceptible he is to suggestions. No matter where you are, if you are observant, you can practice using suggestions and develop ability to use them in hypnosis.

In waking hypnosis we have motivation, expectancy and imagination working. They are aroused by curiosity and the will to experiment. Almost any suggestion will be welcomed that is not repugnant to the moral sense of the person you are working with. The average person likes to feel that he is a part of an experiment if he consents to be hypnotized. Elucidate on this fact before testing or hypnotizing anyone.

THE HYPNOIDAL STATE

Each state of hypnosis has specific values. The name applied to the state refers to the hypnotic condition, the purpose for which it can be used, and the phenomena it can produce. The extraordinary powers of the subconscious mind are tapped through hypnosis and are employed to perform work which the conscious mind seems unable to do. The amount of this power released depends on the depth of hypnosis. The deeper the state of hypnosis, the more extraordinary power can be utilized. The opening into this phenomenal realm of extraordinary power is the hypnoidal state. As we go deeper into hypnosis the opening expands and we are then able to explore further into the amazing and fantastic states of catalepsy and somnambulism.

The word HYPNOIDAL means RESEMBLING SLEEP. The resemblance to sleep exists because the individual's appearance and condition, during hypnosis, is almost identical to one who is asleep. The comparison to sleep ends here. In this state, the conscious mind is awake and able to think, listen and to act, if it so desires. It is capable of accepting or rejecting any suggestions. There are three stages easily recognized. The first stage produces a tired feeling, the second a heavy feeling in the limbs, and the third brings on a drowsy feeling. These can be observed as they appear. We call these the visual signs of hypnosis. The drowsy appearance manifests because of the extreme relaxation produced by the influence of hypnosis.

The imitative appearance of sleep is shown when complete physical and mental tension is released and deep hypnosis has been induced. Genuine sleep, familiar to all of us, is not produced in hypnosis. The suggestion to go into a normal, natural sleep must be given before a hypnotee will go into a natural sleep, as long as the hypnotist has control. Sometimes during the lighter stages of hypnosis, a person will go to sleep, but it is because the hypnotist has lost the rapport, therefore, losing control, allowing the person to enter natural sleep.

The hypnoidal condition allows the hypnotee to do as he pleases, but it enforces suggestions, provides the opportunity to teach him to accept positive suggestions and automatically reject negative ones. This state can be called the TEACHING STATE. Suggestions can be implanted within the mind that will take effect in the future. While in this hypnoidal condition, a person can be taught to inhibit bad habits.

We can re-educated the mind to alter negative opinions and inoculate direct convictions within it. From a therapeutic standpoint, it matters little whether light, medium or deep hypnosis is produced. The depth of hypnosis is important to control amnesia, analgesia and anesthesia, or to implant post hypnotic suggestions. The objectives can be implanted in the mind in the hypnoidal state. The effects of the hypnoidal state can be linked with a day dreaming state of mind. It is also similar to the effects of a sedative which relaxes the nerves without interfering with the conscious mind.

Evaluation of the hypnoidal state shows the conscious mind is more apt to receive educational material because it is more amenable to suggestions. The individual in this condition can be taught to apply conscious will and effort to anything that will be of help to him in any manner. Positive suggestions are a part of the educational material the mind desires so much to absorb and use to advantage. The conscious mind, in the hypnoidal condition, does not wish to be disturbed. It is passive, calm and still, partially inhibited from thinking. Thoughts do not bother it in any way. It is in a state of increased receptivity, ready to receive methodical suggestions.

The individual hypnotized into this condition accelerates the positive action of the suggestions by utilizing his own power of auto suggestion. The conscious and subconscious minds both assimilate the suggestions in this state and work together to achieve one goal. They are encouraged to be perseveringly diligent in the cataleptic state and are incited to attain the goal in the somnambulistic state. In these latter states hypnosis acts as the spur, the stimulus, which unceasingly carries on until the goal is reached.

The hypnoidal condition causes the conscious mind to accede to suggestions, to more or less just listen without interfering. The deeper conditions of hypnosis, such as exist in the cataleptic and somnambulistic states, conditions the subconscious mind to obey. Conscious will and effort are present only in the hynoidal state. Automatic and mechanical obedience is acquired in the deeper states because the will is not active. The imagination has taken its place. But the will can resist and awaken out of the hypnoidal and cataleptic states. Complete control is gained by the hypnotist in somnambulism. This kind of control inhibits the conscious mind from using the will to interfere, allowing the subconscious to comply with suggestions during and after the hypnotic session.

Eighty percent of the people who are hypnotized feel the effects of the hypnoidal condition. When a person first experiences these effects, he seldom will accept the fact that he was hypnotized. Because he has often experienced feelings of being tired, heavy and drowsy, he is unaware that the suggestions have produced these feelings. Until he enters the cataleptic state, where tests for rigidity are applied, he will deny that he was hypnotized and say, "I was not hypnotized, I just relaxed." Words and statements such as this do not come as a surprise to a hypnotist. It is usually expected from most people. Do not be surprised if you try to hypnotize someone and he tells you that he did not feel anything, he just relaxed and waited for something to happen. As long as the hypnotee remains in the hypnoidal state and you have not made him do anything to convince him that he is hypnotized, you will never establish a firm, strong rapport between you. Try to get an arm to levitate, or use the eyelid test to gain more respect and rapport.

How can we tell when a person is influenced by hypnotic suggestions? It is quite easy if you learn to detect the visual signs of hypnosis at work. The very first thing to remember is this: THE MORE SLOW AND SLUGGISH ALL MOVEMENTS, PULSE AND BREATHING, THE DEEPER THE DEPTHS OF HYPNOSIS. The more observant you are to this fact, the better you will be as an operator in the art of hypnotizing. Let us assume that we are trying to induce hypnosis. We begin by talking to him about hypnosis. We call this a PRE-HYPNOTIC TALK or CONSULTATION. It is important that we do this because we want to watch his normal, natural movements, his breathing rate and pulse action. Without taking his pulse, we look at the sides of the neck to see if we can detect a pulsing action in the carotid arteries. We can notice the pulse rate by observing the slight pulsating movement of the foot, as one leg comfortably dangles across the other. We look at the chest and note the rate of breathing, or see the abdomen expanding and contracting as he inhales and exhales. We look at the eyes, their clearness and brightness. The rhythm of the blinking is noted. Every tic and twitch of a muscle anywhere on the face, arms, legs or body is noted. All of his movements are classified in our mind. Which are voluntary and which are not. It is the involuntary movements we must consider. They will tell a story. They will guide us so that we will not make any mistakes, such as saying SLEEP while and when he is wide awake. They are the visual signs we must learn. It is the language of hypnotism spoken in signs from the hypnotee to the hypnotist. Yes, there is a sign language and if you can read the signs well, you will be able to maintain prestige and rapport between you and the person you hypnotize. Now that we have studied the individual and think we can hypnotize him, we tell him, "Place yourself in a more comfortable position with both feet on the floor and let us see if you are able to follow directions." (No mention is made of hypnotizing him.) The intention is to introduce him into hypnosis by producing the hypnoidal condition. We continue as follows: (SLOW AND MONOTONOUS VOICE) "Make yourself as comfortable as you can and relax. Jut relax. Relax, relax, relax. You are just resting and relaxing. In a few moments you will feel pleasantly warm and comfortable. Listen to my voice and let me lead you. Let me guide you. You are going to relax as you have never relaxed before. You will listen to my voice and comply with every suggestion as long as it is good for you and will help you to advance to better yourself and your conditions. You will automatically reject anything negative, harmful, or detrimental to your welfare and well-being. Relax. Rest. Keep on relaxing and resting. Just resting and relaxing more and more with each moment that passes. You are tired. Tired. Getting tired. Your eyelids are becoming heavy. Your arms soon will feel heavy. Your legs, from your thighs down to the bottom of your feet, will both feel so heavy. Relax, relax, relax. Your eyes are tired. Tired. So tired. Your eyelids get heavier. They are so very heavy. They want to close. You will let them close and relax more and more with each breath you take. Keep on resting and relaxing. Relax. Relax. Relax. Rest, rest, rest and just continue to relax. Feeling warm and so very comfortable all over. Your eyelids are so very heavy, you can hardly keep them open. You are very tired, so very tired. Relax, rest, aware of my voice. Always aware of my voice. Just relaxing, relaxing, relaxing. Rest and relax. Your eyelids are closing, closing, they are so heavy, so very heavy, they are closing now. Your arms are relaxing more and more. Every nerve and muscle is relaxing. Your arms get heavy, heavy, heavy, so heavy, just too heavy to move. Relax. Relax. Relax. Your legs are now relaxing as they have never relaxed before and you feel they are relaxing. They are so heavy. Very, very heavy, just too heavy to move. Relax. Relax. Relax. You feel tired all over. Your arms are heavy, your legs are heavy and you just want to relax more and more. It feels so good to do nothing. Just relaxing and resting and becoming more and more tired, heavy and drowsy. So tired, so heavy, so drowsy. Still resting and relaxing. Relaxing as you have never relaxed before. Let yourself go now and just drowsily drift along. Still letting me lead you. Soon you will let yourself go into a soothing delightful sleep. Just for a few moments so that you can enjoy this wonderful feeling longer and awaken feeling refreshed, full of vim, vigor and vitality. Nothing will disturb you. Nothing will bother you. My voice will continue to guide you as you drift away into sleep. You are very drowsy, so very drowsy, tired and drowsy, desiring only to drift away into sleep. Let yourself go and drift, drift, drift into sleep."

The visual signs to watch for are: Positions of the arms, legs and body should be relaxed, comfortable and free of tension. Movements of the fingers, feet, body and other voluntary and involuntary actions should slow up and become still. Breathing and pulse rate changed. Breathing usually slows and continues to do so as the depths of hypnosis increases. The pulse may quicken for a moment or two, but it also will usually slow up. (If pulse rate increases or breathing is too fast or too shallow, it is a sign of fear or hysteria. The person should be immediately brought out of the hypnotic condition, no matter in what stage or state he may be in.)

The eyes show tiredness. They will become void of brightness and either stare into space, not moving, or look sleepy. Sometimes a dull look and watery eyes appear just before the eyelids close. Sometimes the eyes will roam from side to side or tend to roll up. They move slowly or are still. (IF YOU HAVE STUDIED THE ACTION OF THE EYES BEFORE THE INDUCTION INTO HYPNOSIS, YOU WILL HAVE NOTICED THAT THE EYES DID NOT ROAM FROM SIDE TO SIDE. THEY WERE MOVING UP AND DOWN. THE SIDE TO SIDE MOTION IS A SIGN SHOWING THE INDIVIDUAL IS ABOUT TO ENTER CATALEPSY. HE IS GOING FASTER THAN YOUR WORDS SUGGEST. IF THE TENDENCY IS TO ROLL UP INTO THE HEAD, IT IS A SIGN THAT THE HYPNOTEE IS GOING TOO FAST ALTOGETHER, HE IS ON THE VERGE OF SOMNAMBULISM. YOU MUST LEARN HOW TO PICK UP WHERE THE SIGNS LEAD YOU. YOU CANNOT ALWAYS FOLLOW THE PATTER YOU INTEND TO USE. BE READY AT ALL TIMES, TO CHANGE IN ACCORD WITH THE INDIVIDUAL'S ABILITY TO LET HIMSELF GO. IT IS A KNOWN FACT THAT THE SOMNAMBULE, THE BEST TYPE OF PERSON TO BE HYPNOTIZED QUICKLY AND EASILY, WITH THE SNAP OF A FINGER AND THE WORD SLEEP, HAS FOUND THE SECRET OF FORGETTING HIMSELF INSTANTLY. WATCH FOR THIS TYPE OF PERSON. YOU MUST FOLLOW HIM. HE WILL NOT FOLLOW YOU.

The eyelids show signs of being heavy and they begin to close and flutter as soon as the hypnotee is in hypnosis. Before they close entirely, the rhythm of opening and closing has changed and can be easily seen. The look on the face will change to one of being tired and drowsy. The look takes on the appearance of feeling drowsy when the eyelids feel too heavy to keep open. Usually the lips remain closed for a while. But as the depth of hypnosis increases, they will open slightly or else you will see the lower jaw drop. This is a sign showing complete physical relaxation has been attained. Mental tension is released in catalepsy. It is the next state the hypnotee will enter.

The effect we endeavor to produce within the mind of a hypnotee depends on the kind of suggestions we use in the patter. The opiate effect of the monotonous voice renders assistance to the incredulous mind causing it to become more amenable to suggestions. As the depth of hypnosis increases, we become aware of the fact that, SUGGESTIONS PROPERLY WORDED AND APPLIED IN KEEPING WITH THE HYPNOTEE'S LIKES AND DESIRES WILL ACT AS A SEDATIVE TO THE BRAIN AND PRODUCE THE EFFECTS AND RESULTS WE DESIRE TO COME ABOUT.

The sensations experienced by those who have been in the hypnoidal state are variously described. But most hypnotees agree that after the eyes close, a drowsy feeling follows. Sometimes it is accompanied with a sensation of heaviness, lightness or tingling over the body. Some experience sensations of falling asleep, others feel suspended in air, light as a feather and walking on air, or floating on a cloud. Others have described sensations of leaving the body, dreaming, and some have been unable to feel anything but a pleasant, soothing sensation of calmness. Some have been aware of muscles twitching, swallowing hard, pulse racing, breathing faster or slower, etc. But, none mention any unpleasant feeling or sensation experienced while in any state of hypnosis.

The hypnoidal condition only slightly influences the individual. He is just tired and drowsy and can withstand the sleep suggestions and come out of it at any time. But informative suggestions and instructional material can be intrenched firmly on the conscious mind.

The next phase of hypnosis is the CATALEPTIC STATE. That which can be done in this state is truly phenomenal.

THE CATALEPTIC STATE

Some researchers in hypnotism believe that hypnosis was used in biblical times. They say that the staff of Moses was a snake turned cataleptic by the use of animal magnetism. We know that the name Magnetism was changed to Hypnotism and also know that reference to magnetism is in the bible as well as in many of the books dealing with religion and ancient magic, witchcraft, psychic phenomena and spiritism. Some researchers believe that the first post hypnotic phenomena is revealed in the story of how Lot's wife was turned to a pillar of stone. Other beliefs are the feeding of 100 men with 20 loaves of barley by the prophet, Elisha, and the feeding of the 5000 with 5 loaves and two fishes by Jesus Christ. These could have been accomplished with hypnosis. We feel that this information in reference to research work may help you to understand that as far back as the history of man is recorded, there is reference to the power of hypnosis (the power of suggestion or magnetism). We feel that there have always been master hypnotists in every civilization. References to cataleptic conditions can be found through research, thus revealing that hypnosis was a part of the metaphysical sciences of the past.

This phase of hypnosis has been well named. In this state, scientifically called the CATALEPTIC STATE, Extraordinary Hypnotic Phenomena (EHP) can well be demonstrated. The demonstration of catalepsy, produced through hypnosis, is usually the climax to most stage and night club hypnotic performances. A person who has been hypnotized is placed between two chairs with the head on one and the heels on another, letting the body be suspended in the air, acting as a bridge between the two chairs. The body remains stiff and rigid. It is not unusual to see one or two people sitting on the body while it is in that position, without bending from the added weight. This is a phenomena which is produced by hypnotic suggestions. The hypnotic condition which exists in the body and mind of the hypnotee is of such nature, that it can manifest itself by causing the muscles of the body to become stiff and rigid, as stone or steel. In this state, the hypnotist has control of muscular activity. Every muscle within the body can be controlled by using the proper hypnotic suggestions while a person is in the state of catalepsy.

Catalepsy is the borderline between wakefulness and sleep. When the hypnotee enters this state, a deeper degree of sleep and a stronger rapport are established. The hypnotist acquires more control as the depth of hypnosis is increased. But in all stages of catalepsy only partial control is gained. There are three stages easily identified by tests. The first stage demonstrates partial control of thoughts and movements. The visual signs are the immobility of movements, (all movements have ceased) and the hypnotee's attention is centered on the hypnotist. In order to be sure that the hypnotee is in this first stage, an arm is raised almost to shoulder height and held for a few moments by the hypnotist. He holds it up by a hand which is placed directly under the elbow and then removes the hand after suggesting to the hypnotee that it will remain suspended in the air. He is told that he cannot move or lower it, no matter how hard he tries to lower it, he will not be able to do so. If he cannot move or lower the arm, he is in the first stage. He can awaken from this stage if he desires but not as easy as he can from the hypnoidal state. He must use some effort, and if he succeeds he will usually deny that he was hypnotized.

The second stage demonstrates partial control over muscular activity. The visual signs are a sleepy look and the attitude of a body completely relaxed and free of all tension. Sometimes the head droops to the side, the eyes can be seen to roam from side to side or remain still for long periods of time. The breathing is slower. An opening appears in the lips, or the mouth will open slightly. If an arm is made to swing along the side of the body, it will look like it was made of rubber, flexible and waxy. The test for this stage is controlling muscular action by making an arm hard, stiff and rigid, like a bar of steel. If we can accomplish this, we are certain that the hypnotee is in the second stage. We apply the test when we have the arm raised in the first stage and find that the hypnotee has not been able to move or lower it. We take the arm again, holding it under the elbow with one hand and the wrist with the other, we pull on it gently and slowly, suggesting that the arm is getting hard, stiff and rigid. After a few moments, we can feel the muscles become hard and stiff. We then let go and challenge him to try to bend it. If he cannot, he is in the second stage. Releasing the hard, stiff and rigid condition by countermanding the suggestions which produced this effect, we endeavor to induce him to go deeper, into the next stage.

The third stage demonstrates control of automatic movements and partial control of amnesia, analgesia and anesthesia. If the hands are made to revolve around each other; or made to shake and quiver; or an arm is made to rotate in circular fashion, the movement will continue automatically until it is stopped by the hypnotist. This is an exhibition of automatism which is characteristic of the third stage. As rigidity is the characteristic of the second stage and automatism of the third, we have, in the deeper degree of catalepsy NEARING THE BORDERLINE OF SOMNAMBUL-ISM, partial control of amnesia, analgesia and an-esthesia. Also characteristic of the third stage is the ability to partially control feelings and sensations, but only on the surface of the body.

After attaining a stiff and rigid arm, the next test to apply is one that will show that we have control of automatic movement. As stated above, we make the hands or an arm go around and around and tell the hypnotee that he cannot stop them from moving that way. No matter how hard he will try to stop them, they will continue to go faster and faster, until he is told to stop. If they continue to move and DO GO FASTER WHEN HE TRIES TO STOP, then he is deep in the third stage. If he tries to stop and the movement begins to slow up or stop, and the hands or arm still remain in position, he is still in the second stage. If they drop down to the lap or side of the body, he is DEHYPNO-TIZING HIMSELF and trying to awaken. In this latter case, the hypnotist should endeavor to induce the hypnotee to rest and relax. Encouraging the hypnotee by suggesting that it will be better to rest and relax and sleep for awhile, will generally keep him from awakening. A few moments of listening to suggestions of this kind, "You will soon awaken, very refreshed, completely relaxed and free from all worries and cares, etc." will often turn the mind to accept further suggestions of going deeper.

Assuming that the hypnotee has not been able to stop the movement and we know we have attained immobility, rigidity and automatism, the next step would be to try to find out the degree of hypnosis present. Determining the depth of hypnosis from now on is the most important thing and very vital to our ability to produce extraordinary phenomena. Until this stage we have been introduced into the surface phenomena. Everything has been produced on the outside of the body of the hypnotee. We now begin to explore into the realm of the senses and see what hypnosis can produce from within the body.

The third stage of catalepsy is often mistaken for somnambulism. But the characteristics of catalepsy are not the same as those in somnambulism as we shall see later. The resemblance to somnambulism lies in the ability to produce anesthesia in the hand (this is known as a glove anesthesia) and because some post hypnotic suggestions can be effectively carried out. Most hypnotists forget that partial control exists in catalepsy or else are not aware of this being a CHIEF CHARACTERISTIC of catalepsy. Post hypnotics are usually carried out in a delayed time or are not carried out at all because of this factor. The hypnotee sometimes will remark that he knows that he is supposed to do something and at a given time, but he will refuse to comply because the control was not complete. another factor involved in post hypnotics not being carried out is that the hypnotee was not told to carry out the suggestion just before the awakening. The post hypnotic should be repeated at least three times as the last thing to be given. As an example: "When I tell you to awaken, you will immediately open your eyes and awaken. You will, on awakening, go to the door and open it and then go back to your seat and relax." (Repeated twice) "Listen very carefully to the following suggestion. Pay close attention and when you awaken, you will obey and comply with the suggestion you are about to hear." The above post hypnotic is then repeated again followed by the words, "WAKE UP! OPEN YOUR EYES AND AWAKEN!" Because partial amnesia is present in the cataleptic state, it interferes with post hypnotics unless they are the last things a hypnotee hears before he awakens. Many times the post hypnotics are given in the lighter stages of catalepsy and forgotten to be repeated before the awakening. The third stage of catalepsy, being over the border and almost in the realm of sleep, allows the subconscious to come forth and establish relationship with the hypnotist. A more direct and firm rapport then exists between the hypnotee and the hypnotist. It is, at this time, that complete attention of the subconscious mind is attained. If the fundamental principals of hypnosis are present and working within the hypnotee, he will go deeper into the somnambulistic state and obey every suggestion, giving complete control to the hypnotist. The fundamental principals will be in a later chapter.

There is partial control of amnesia, analgesia and anesthesia in catalepsy and tests are applied to find out whether they are present. The test for amnesia is to tell a hypnotee that he cannot speak his name. He is told that he has forgotten it. Almost anything that he remembers well, can be temporarily forgotten if he is told that he does not remember it. If he does not remember when he attempts to recall what it is that you have told him to forget or not be able to remember, you can be certain he is in the third stage. Partial amnesia has taken effect and is working.

To test for analgesia, the hypnotee is told that he will feel no sensation when you touch his hand. The back of the hand is then pinched or a fingernail is moved across it. He is asked if he feels anything. If he does not, he is in the third stage and anesthesia can be tested. This is done immediately after the analgesia test is over, by telling the hypnotee that the hand is numb and all feelings and sensations are gone. There will be no sign of movement or contracting of muscles if the hand is stuck with a needle or is pinched very hard. If the test proves that there isn't any feelings or sensations, a glove anesthesia has been produced. If the hypnotee is on the border of somnambulism or in that state, the anesthetic effect can be transferred to other parts of the body by placing the hand there and telling the hypnotee that the area is now numb and anesthetized. If the area is found to be anesthetized after testing for pain, then the hypnotee is in the first stage of somnambulism or deeper.

The third stage of catalepsy also can produce partial hallucinations. This can be proven by the fact that many hypnotees will perform and act as though they have or have not seen the object when a negative or positive hallucination is suggested. But when questioned will say they saw the object, yet the mind wouldn't accept the fact that it was there. As an example: A handbag or glass of water is held in the hand of another person and the hypnotee is told that the person is leaving. Immediately the hypnotee will see the handbag or glass of water standing alone in the air. This is a negative hallucination. The person holding the object has disappeared as if by magic and only the object remains to be seen. But, the hypnotee will usually laugh at this because he does see the person yet is unable to cope with the fact that the mind will not accept it. In the somnambulistic state the hypnotee will see only the object and not the person. He will not laugh nor will he argue about it. If you ask him to describe what he sees, he will tell you that he sees the object. If you insist that the person is also present, he may tell you to have your eyes examined because there is no one there holding the object. It is just there and that is all there is to it. He will stand steadfast and nothing can change his mind about it.

It is advisable to question the hypnotee after the awakening, in regards to hallucinations. By the answers, you can tell whether he was in catalepsy or in somnambulism. If he remembers all of it, he was in the second stage. If he can only recall part of it, he was in the third stage and partial amnesia was in effect. If he cannot recall any of it, he was in somnambulism, as complete amnesia was in effect. The questioning in this case acts as a test for efficiency in carrying out a hypnotic hallucination and to verify the condition and state of hypnosis. The depth of hypnosis can always be judged by questioning a hypnotee after the awakening from hypnosis.

You must imprint this fact on your mind. The chief characteristics of catalepsy are PARTIAL CONTROL and RIGIDITY. We have partial control of muscular activity because we do not have control of the bodily muscles. We do have complete control of the muscles in the limbs, but it is to be remembered that it is in the limbs only and not in the body.

What are the advantages of working in the cataleptic state? The ability to use rigidity in cases involving burns and broken, fractured bones so that movement does not interfere with the healing process. This advantage is being used in the field of medicine. The ability to produce anesthesia on a part of the body without drugs is used in medicine and dentistry, allowing for minor surgery to be performed to the advantage of the doctor, dentist and the patient as well. One of the books in this series of LIVING WITH HYPNOSIS will be on medical hypnosis, another will be on hypnotherapy. Within these books will be the information on how these advantages and other cataleptic conditions are used today.

Other advantages of catalepsy as used in psychology, optometry, chiropractics, etc., will also be forthcoming in books of this series. It would take too many pages and too much time to relate all of the advantages in one book. It is better to divulge the right information to those who are interested in specific fields, in a book written for that specialty. We will endeavor to do this with the hope that they will use the information to great advantage to themselves and their clients. We have gone through the state of catalepsy, we shall now continue on to the somnambulistic state.

THE SOMNAMBULISTIC STATE

THERE ARE TWO KINDS OF SOMNAMBUL-ISM—NATURAL AND ARTIFICIAL.
The phenomena manifested in this state is of subconscious origin and extraordinary in nature. The exploits of sleep-walkers are well known. The sleep-walker, in a state of somnambulism, is able to perform phenomenal feats. He has the ability to produce this condition but cannot control it without the help of a hypnotist. This is NATURAL somnambulism. Through hetero hypnosis we produce ARTIFICIAL somnambulism and maintain control of the subconscious at all times. This is one of the reasons why self hypnosis is difficult to achieve. As we cannot take time to go into this further, the book on SELF HYPNOSIS, the second in the series of LIVING WITH HYPNOSIS, will provide more information on how to attain self hypnotic control.

A hypnotee entering the state of somnambulism, automatically and mechanically responds to suggestions. The body and the senses can be controlled. As stated before, there are three states classified as hypnotic, qualified by hetero control. They are the Hypnoidal, Cataleptic and Somnambulistic states. Beyond somnambulism there are three trance states seldom recognized or identified with hypnosis, the Comatose, Catatonic and Suspended Animation. We become involved in these trance states when working with medical hypnosis, hypnotherapy, psychic phenomena and metaphysical hypnosis. A hypnotee may enter into a trance state momentarily. During that time there is no hetero control. Many times in deep hypnosis, an individual will not respond for a while and then will resume complying with suggestions. Here we have temporary conditions existing in the comatose state. When hetero control is lost, in deep hypnosis, if after awakening, the hypnotee remarks that he was elsewhere or in the past, (regressed) we can identify this condition as being catatonic. In the United States, we need not concern ourselves with suspended animation as this condition is seldom found to exist any longer since embalming became a law. Prior to this century, people were buried alive due to the condition of suspended animation which resembled death. When exhumed some were found suffocated and their bodies were in positions other than in repose. Suspended animation is practiced only in yoga, etc.

The moment a hypnotee enters the first stage of somnambulism, the conscious mind is suppressed. The subconscious is free from physical awareness and open to receive the communicating link which binds it to the hypnotist. This is the patter of the hypnotist, the suggestions and words which it first hears and becomes aware of in the hypnoidal state. The link is secured by the rapport established as the depth of hypnosis increases. In the somnambulistic state, the line of communication is open and all of the interfering factors have been taken care of. Complete control is gained and maintained until the line is closed and the hypnotee is awakened. But arrangements are made before the closing of the line at this first contact. A signal of some kind is arranged to enable the hypnotist to contact the subconscious immediately without going through the hypnoidal and cataleptic states. By this post hypnotic signal, the hypnotist can, at any time, make immediate contact with the subconscious under any circumstance and control its action from the moment contact is made.

As long as the patter or the voice of the hypnotist continues to go on, control can be maintained and natural sleep avoided. On reaching this state, some hypnotees will go into a natural sleep if not spoken to. A natural somnambule has the ability to forget himself. The hypnotee must be able to do the same thing if he desires to go into deep hypnosis. Those who are able to forget themselves quickly enter this state more readily. Those who have good control of themselves and can withdraw their minds from their surroundings and fix their attention determinedly on the hypnotist, can also reach this state with ease. While in this state, they hear and will speak to the person into whose care they have entrusted themselves, and no one else. The senses are at rest. They will respond only to the hypnotist. He has complete control. If he directs the hypnotee not to do so, no one else can arouse them to see, hear, touch, taste or smell. Because the control is so complete, the senses can be directed to become supernormal. We therefore, have a condition in somnambulism which allows the subconscious mind to use all of its powers or inhibit them from working entirely. The organs within the body can be controlled as easily as the senses. They can be regulated to function normally, faster or slower. This phenomenal condition, controlled by a hypnotist, performs the wondrous extraordinary things we hear so much about. More about the senses and the organs will be published later, since these subjects are not related to the present matter at hand.

How can you tell when a person is in the first stage of somnambulism? If you will recall what the visual signs of catalepsy are and know the tests to apply in that state, you will remember that the last thing we did was to test for automatism and partial amnesia and anesthesia. The automatic action continued until it was stopped by the hypnotist. The amnesia test showed that he could not recall what he was told to forget. The glove anesthesia showed partial or local insensibility of feelings, sensation and pain. This was accomplished in the third stage of catalepsy.

We may assume that a hypnotee is in the somnambulistic state and want to know if we are right. The first stage will show complete control of the senses, partial control of internal feelings and sensations, and complete amnesia on awakening. The second stage will show the senses to be supernormal, feelings and sensations super-sensitized and the hypnotee will react to hallucinations and perform psychically. He will also manifest control of every organ within his body. He will obey and comply perfectly with post hypnotic suggestions, orders or commands. At all times during the third stage, the hypnotee will not do anything unless he is told to do so by the hypnotist. Complete control can be passed to another person in the third stage. In the lighter stages if control is passed to another without the consent of the hypnotee, he can, with determined effort and will, dehypnotize himself. The hypnotee in the third stage, will look and act as if he is in a trance.

All movements and bodily functions are slow and sluggish, manifesting as though they are drugged or asleep. The hypnotee must be told that every part of him is functioning normally as soon as he enters the third stage or else he may not wish to awaken when he is told to wake up. He will remain as long as he can in this complete state of relaxation where no tension of any kind exists.

The first test for somnambulism is to have the hypnotee open his eyes without waking up. We watch closely as he does so and we see that he seems to have trouble opening them. We encourage him to open them, telling him that he CAN open his eyes. The procedure for testing follows:

"When I tell you to do so, without awakening, you will open your eyes. You may find it a little difficult to do so, but you will open your eyes without waking up. OPEN YOUR EYES!"

Watch the hypnotee carefully. You will notice the forehead raise with the attempt to open the eyes, or no attempt will be made at all. In either case, encourage him to open the eyes. When they are open, they will have a glassy look, stare straight ahead, or look upward. They will not move, nor will the eyelids blink for long periods of time. Sometimes the eyes will give the impression, to an observer, of the person drugged or in a trance. The hypnotee is told that the eyes will not dilate or contract, that they will remain undisturbed and uneffected by any light. A light beam from a flashlight (a penlight is usually used) or the flame of a match or candle is passed before the eyes. If the hypnotee is in somnambulism, he will show no response to the light. The eye or both eyes will not dilate or contract. If one eyelid is closed, it will remain closed until opened by the hypnotist, either through suggestion or by placing his thumb on the eyelid and lifting it up. If the eyes do not respond to any light and the eyelid can be closed, the sense of sight is now completely controlled.

The next step is to test for control of hearing. We do this in many ways. The best way is to tell the hypnotee that he will not allow anything to disturb, bother or upset him in any way. He is told that no sound or noise will bother him no matter what the sound or noise will be. That he will hear only your voice and nothing else until he is told that he will hear everything in a normal manner. The hands are then clapped together to make a very loud sound like the bursting of a paper bag blown up and smashed between the hands. The procedure follows:

"Listen very carefully. From now on you hear my voice and my voice only. No other sound or noise will bother or disturb you in any way. Your ears have shut off all other sounds and noises. My voice is the only sound you hear. No matter what the sound or noise will be, no matter how loud the sound or noise, it will not matter to you. As far as you are concerned there is no other sound. You hear my voice and my voice only, from now on, until I tell you that you can hear normally and naturally. No other sound will effect you in any way." THE HANDS ARE THEN CLAPPED TOGETHER ONCE, LOUDLY AND QUICKLY. If there is no response to the loud noise and you have not seen any movement of the eyes, eyelids or raising of the brow or any movement of the body, the sense of hearing is controlled. To check to be sure, we take our index finger and touch the corner of the eye and watch for any movement. We touch the ear and watch the eye area. If there is no response to the touch, he is in somnambulism and two senses are controlled. You can touch the eye itself and no response will be obtained in this state.

We have the hypnotee in the first stage and know that we can control the sense of sight and hearing. We are certain about the condition the hypnotee is in when he responds to imaginary stimuli. Therefore, a hallucination will show us the exact degree and condition of hypnosis by the visual signs we detect. This determines which of the senses are being used by the subconscious in complying with our suggestions. If we can reverse all of the senses or counteract the natural way they function, we are very sure that we are working in the somnambulistic state.

We are now interested in knowing whether we can cause the olfactory nerves (sense of smell) to become completely void of the ability to respond to anything other than what we might suggest. The idea is to see if we can make the olfactory nerves obey and comply with our hallucinary suggestions. We can use a variety of things and either make it non-existing, which is a negative hallucination, or use nothing at all and suggest that it does exist, which is a positive hallucination. By using anything as strong as ammonia (or smelling salts) and suggesting that it is something else, or non-existant, we are able to produce the visual signs we desire so much to recognize. We are certain that the sense of smell is controlled if the hypnotee does not flinch away from the ammonia (or smelling salts). This gives definite proof that he is not faking.

We are also certain the olfactory nerves are controlled if we suggest that the ammonia is the fragrance of roses (any flower) and he shows signs of enjoying the smell as you pass the container of ammonia under his nose. The procedure for testing the olfactory nerves generally is as follows:

"Keep on resting, just relax and go deeper into sleep. As you continue to listen to my voice you become aware of a fragrant odor in the room. It smells like roses. Yes, it is the pleasant fragrance from the roses in this room. You can smell it now! It is a clean, delightful odor. Getting stronger. Let me bring one of the roses to you. Here it is. It is a beautiful rose and smells so good. (THE CONTAINER WITH AMMONIA IS PASSED BACK AND FORTH UNDER THE NOSE.

We now go on to determine whether we can control the sense of taste. The gustatory nerves respond to imaginary things very easily. The squeezing of a lemon before our eyes causes these nerves to respond quickly. We provide the hypnotee with suggestions that effect these nerves in the same manner as when using a lemon or anything else which may effect this sense. Swallowing is a part of this sense. In the somnambulistic state swallowing almost ceases, therefore, we try to make the hypnotee feel things which will cause him to swallow. The salivary glands respond to stimuli such as the lemon we mentioned above. If we can control the salivary glands, swallowing and the actual taste buds on the tongue, we have the ability to control portions of the body that function when we eat or drink. This tells us that we are slowly proceeding to control the hypnotee's organs, glands, etc. We do the same thing with the sense of taste as we have done with the other three senses before. In all tests, it is advisable to use a hallucinary suggestion to cause the imagination to work for us and to prove that we have control by using something that will effect the hypnotee in the same manner as if he were wide awake and in a normal and natural, physical and mental condition. In the case of testing for proof of control, the hypnotee can be made to eat an onion or potato as though it were an apple or any other kind of fruit. The main idea is to find out whether the hypnotee is faking or is in deep hypnosis.

The chief reason for testing for proof of control is to avoid embarrassing situations and harmful effects.

A good example of controlling taste lies in controlling the habit of eating, drinking (alcoholism), smoking and any other habit of this nature where the taste buds are involved. A smoker is told that a cigarette will taste bad, unpleasant, or something of the sort. An excessive eater can be told that candy or chocolates, pies and pastries, etc. will no longer appeal to him and he can be given a multitude of reasons and causes, or he can be told that they will taste horrible to him or make him nauseous. A drinker can be told that he will not be able to hold the liquor, etc.

The sense of touch is likewise to be tested for control. The tactile nerves will respond quite easily and quickly to a pinch, the prick of a pin or to anything that is hot or very cold. If the hypnotee is told that he will feel no pain and he is pinched, etc., he will show no sign of feeling pain if he is in the somnambulistic state. We mentioned before that in catalepsy anesthesia can be controlled. But, the difference between the type of control that exists in these two states is that in catalepsy we have surface control, whereas, in this state we have a deeper and more penetrating control. A hypnotee can be told that he will feel no pain internally in a specified area and there will be no pain if he is in any stage in this state. Major surgery can be performed. In the cataleptic state only minor surgery can be performed. This is to be remembered at all times.

After the senses are controlled and we are certain that we can control them, we endeavor to determine the depth of control. How deep into the anatomy can we go with our hypnotic control? We try to produce an effect of some kind which will show visual signs exhibiting the effect we desire to obtain. We know that we have controlled the senses and are certain that we are in the first stage of somnambulism. If we can control feelings and sensations from within the hypnotee, we will know that we have gone deeper into hypnosis. The second stage demonstrates control of feelings and sensations produced from the internal systems within the body. The next step is to control the pulse, respiration and temperature. If we can do this, we will be certain that we are in the second stage or deeper.

We start with respiration and control the rhythm of

breathing. The hypnotee is told that he is relaxing and is free from every bit of tension within the body. The breathing rate is controlled by stating or suggesting that he is now breathing too fast or too slow. Watch to see if the rate of breathing changes and whether or not it will continue as suggested. If this is accomplished and control of breathing is obtained, we try to control the temperature by suggesting that the room is stuffy and too warm. We suggest that it is getting hot and almost unbearable. We suggest that he feels it and is beginning to perspire, or we can suggest the exact opposit and say that it is too cold and that he is now shivering with cold. If he responds to these suggestions, it is certain that he is responding internally. He can be made to laugh or cry, feel happy or sad. In this condition he can be told to open his eyes and act in a normal and natural way and no one would know that he was hypnotized. He would respond and not allow anything to bother or disturb him emotionally or in any other way, if he were told that nothing will upset him during this period.

The pulse rate can be changed by suggesting that he is running away from something or running to get somewhere in a hurry to meet an appointment or the like. Working in accord with the suggestions, his imagination will produce the same effect on him as though he actually were running, yet he would not be taking a single step. When the emotions and the internal systems of the body become involved and exhibit signs of responding to suggestions, it is certain that the hypnotee is in deep somnambulism. The third stage has been reached. In this stage of somnambulism, clairvoyant powers can be demonstrated. Psychic phenomena can be produced. Extra sensory perception of the senses can be exhibited. As examples: Some somnambulistic hypnotees can discern objects hidden in boxes, perceive things a long distance away, hear distantly, smell and taste things in boxes and bottles unlabeled and disguised. They can describe pictures behind them, read cards face down, choose specific objects, cards, etc. from many mixed together. They can read a printed page and recall every word and repeat them when shown a blank page and told that it is the same page they have been reading.

Some somnambulists can see within a person's body. It is true that there are only a few who can. But, the fact remains that it can be done! Some somnambules have the ability to feel things going on within another person's body. They are able to exhibit and demonstrate all of the signs and symptoms of sickness and disease, and can see and feel broken bones, disturbed organs, malfunctioning nerves, muscles, etc.

In this state of somnambulism, psychic phenomena are well demonstrated. The tactile sense is remarkable in distinguishing articles, whether by contact or at a distance. Articles handled by somnambulists can be returned to their rightful owners without ever having seen the articles or the owners before. By impression or feeling of something peculiar they are able to recognize and restore the articles to the owners. Some somnambules can tell the quality, size, shape, or texture, etc., of articles placed at a distance. They can tell the temperature of solids, liquids or things in different places and in other rooms, independent of ever having previous knowledge of them.

Somnambulism is of tremendous value to medical science. A portion of the body can be kept in this condition, independent of the rest and indefinitely. The ability to do this is very useful, extremely so in cases of injury. A hypnotee can be relieved from pain which he otherwise would be obliged to suffer until a physician could be obtained. After an operation, a hypnotee can be awakened, with the exception of the affected part where surgery was performed, so that no pain may be experienced during the time necessary for its complete restoration. In dentistry, a tooth can be extracted in this state and the hypnotee will not miss it, or feel the cavity which has been created by the extraction. The tongue, as is usually the case, is not thrust into the cavity and the unpleasant feelings generally present by the loss of a tooth are not experienced.

The most interesting phenomena of somnambulism is the way post-hypnotic suggestions are worked out to perfection; the complete loss of memory of the events during hypnosis; the ability to regress into the past; and the extraordinary kind of sleep an individual enters into on reaching this state. He is asleep, yet is well able to perform any act or do anything suggested to him whether it is a normal and natural thing, a hallucination, illusion, delusion, etc.

Whether the hypnotee is in a normal condition when he is carrying out a post-hypnotic, or in hypnosis is debatable. It is a matter of dispute as some show signs of knowing what they are doing, but do not know why they are doing it. Some hypnotees appear to be in an abstract frame of mind during the performance of post-hypnotics. Some show signs of having returned into somnambulism momentarily when the post-hypnotic takes effect, especially when a specific time is given to carry out the suggestions. Some will recall what they have done after it is over and wonder why they did such a thing. Post-hypnotic suggestions given in the somnambulistic state can either be carried out immediately after the awakening, or some time later, or after a long period of time such as weeks, months or even years later. It depends on the amount of hypnotic sessions and the kind of training the individual has had in hypnosis. Post-hypnotics should be repeated a few times before the awakening to be certain the hypnotee understands what he is to do. If we wish to ascertain that the hypnotee will carry out the post-hypnotic, we have him verbally repeat the post-hypnotic suggestion prior to the awakening.

Many individuals cannot enter this state easily, especially in the first trial and particularly when they are laboring under pain. With diligent practice they can do so, eventually and with ease. In the practice of self hypnosis those who have the ability to enter this condition at any time, have found it to be a blessing and exercise it at pleasure. Those who do not avail themselves of this blessing to mankind are slaves to prejudice, superstition, ignorance or bigotry and unnecessarily suffer from pain, sickness and disease, as well as from physical and mental tension.

Volumes can be written on the stages and states of hypnosis. Suffice to say, that which is important to this work is herein written. If the reader is interested in the deeper phases of hypnosis and its many uses, phenomenon, etc., the other books in the series of LIVING WITH HYPNOSIS will provide him with information equal to things of interest to him. The world of hypnosis is truly a world of magic and it is there for all to share to better themselves and gain the many blessings it has to offer.

PATTER

What is patter? A patter consists of words and suggestions which are used to induce a condition of hypnosis. The reason why it is called a patter professionally, is because of the manner the words are spoken. The falling rain, the drip of a leaky faucet, the steady hum of a motor, the clicking wheels of a train or anythings that goes on continuously in a monotonous way and effects our senses making us feel drowsy and sleepy, can be construed as a patter. They hypnotize a person by repetition, the ability to cause us to inhibit our senses, motivation and awareness. The words of a hypnotist, during hypnosis, do the same thing. They cause the senses to respond to the suggestions which usually refer to conditions of relaxation, tiredness, a drowsy feeling or sensations of sleep.

The more adept you are in using words and suggestions which affect the senses, the better you will be as a hypnotist. The purpose in using patters is to secure a hold on the subconscious with words that are conducive to success, in establishing rapport. In order to accomplish this, the conscious mind must be soothed into accepting the suggestions to rest, relax and sleep, or induce it to still the thoughts which constantly ramble through the mind. The monotonous way in which a hypnotist works to induce hypnosis usually will get results especially when other quick methods have failed. Whether it be a few words or many words and suggestions monotonously spoken for a long period of time, as long as it is used to hypnotize one or more people, it is called a patter. By using this word PAT-TER, we are enabled to classify the kind of words to use for specific purposes. A medical patter differs from that of a dental patter. All patters are made up of words that are related to the individual hypnotist's vocation or profession. The terminology in patters depends on the kind of results we seek to achieve. It also is in keeping with the kind of words the hypnotee understands.

When hypnosis is induced and a deep stage or degree has been reached, the terminology does not matter too much. The subconscious mind has the ability to understand what the conscious mind does not. It also has the ability to translate languages during hypnosis, and comply with the suggestions given to it. Whether this is done because of the hypnosis, or because the subconscious becomes the psyche itself during hypnosis and is able to translate the hypnotists thoughts and words telepathically or through the senses, is yet unknown. Future experiments may disclose how it is done.

One thing we do know, that the subconscious can produce more psychic phenomena during hypnosis than at any other time. There are conditions of hypnosis, self induced in psychics, which manifests phenomena. It is produced by the patter they practice on themselves which causes the subconscious to dominate consciousness and to obey the thoughts which have been implanted within it during a waking state. Words and suggestions run through our minds all day long. When certain words and suggestions plague us or bombard us and we cannot seem to get rid of them, we are involved in a patter running through our minds and will, sooner or later, do something about it. In this way we are using a form of light self hypnosis. If we make up our minds to do something and diligently obey, making every effort to succeed, we have accepted our own suggestions and carry them out post-hypnotically. Yet we deny ourselves this power by thinking it is our will we use and never realize that we are hypnotizing ourselves. The worries and cares which constantly go on in our minds are patters. They effect us and cause us to respond one way or another, either through deliberately doing something about them externally or we let them affect our body internally and become mentally sick.

The chief condition the patter produces is inhibition of consciousness, which is the first requisite in producing a hypnotic effect. The conscious mind is limited and centered on the hypnotist because of the patter and what it can do. The patter must have words and suggestions which readily make the hypnotee obey. When the conscious mind is in complete abeyance to suggestions the subconscious immediately becomes aware of the voice of the hypnotist and is held almost spellbound during hypnosis. Strong suggestions will generally induce a quick hypnosis. It may or may not be a deep one. The authoritative tone of voice is used only when necessary and on stage for entertainment purposes. For therapy, the soothing tone suggesting that relaxation and tension release will soon overtake the hypnotee will induce a deeper hypnosis. It has also been found that the depth of hypnosis can be more easily increased by using suggestions, repetitiously applied, soothingly in a monotonous manner. Gradual methods used day after day will produce results where other methods fail. Repetition of the suggestions and the length of time involved in inducing hypnosis by gradually training the individual to accept what he is told, is certain to succeed. There are all kinds of methods. None are tried and proven to be more successful than others. It is up to the type of individual and how susceptible he is to suggestions. If he is suggestible, he can be taught to accept hypnotic suggestions.

The principal thing to remember in your patter is to use words in the suggestions which will create the condition you desire the hypnotee to feel. After the induction into hypnosis has been accomplished and the hypnotee is in the proper state, the suggestions used should be ones that will inspire the imagination and will to respond. Curative and therapeutic suggestions are effective when the individual has the inspiration and the desire to get well. Educational suggestions are effective when the conscious mind is still, quiet and calm and is listening to the patter in the same way that the individual would be if he were awake and listening to a classroom lecture. The words in all patters should be to the liking of the individual. The suggestions should be inspiring to him, to awaken a psychological desire to allow them to become a part of his nature, as though they were his own words and coming from within himself. If this is achieved the hypnotee will gain what he desires and will aspire to succeed.

The first time an individual is hypnotized, the patter is the important thing to him. He is concentrating on what he is told. The conscious mind is very alert to the words. The suggestions have little effect because they are not meant to be a part of the conscious mind. It is the subconscious mind we desire to cause to become active and comply with the suggestions. Therefore, the patter should not be full of words that imply a quick and easy result will be obtained. It should convey to the conscious mind that it need not listen too attentively and all that is required of it is to be still and not interfere with what is going on. The suggestions in the patter for hypnotizing anyone for the first time should infer the fact that all you want to do is to relax the body and release the physical and mental tension that is existing presently. If the individual is susceptible and goes into hypnosis quickly and easily, the suggestions can be changed to suit the need or purpose for which the person is being hypnotized. If the individual is able to accept your suggestions of relaxing, resting, etc., and responds, although it may be slow, a change in patter will often hasten the induction and a deeper degree of hypnosis will be attained.

Many times it is advisable to change patters as well as the method of induction. At times a different technique used with an old method will turn the tide to your advantage. It is the patter which counts . . . how you use it . . . what you say . . . and what you do while you are inducing the person to respond. These are the elements which insure a successful induction into deep hypnosis.

The first basic in making up patters is the use of indirect suggestions. After the individual being hypnotized begins to respond to indirect suggestions, they can be changed and direct suggestions can be used. Any person wide awake and alert, scarcely will respond to direct suggestions. No one likes to be told what to do. But when the mind is calm and consciousness is fixed on something holding its attention, the dislike of being forced to do anything does not exist. The patter, therefore, should include such things as a suggestion to mentally picture something good or something which will arouse the memory to bring forth a happy image or thought of the occasion. While the individual is concentrating on this, the indirect suggestions to rest, relax, and loosen every nerve and muscle are in the context of the patter. Words should be used that have one meaning, if possible, so that the individual will not become confused. Suggestions during the first trial should indicate that the results will come later. An example of a patter to induce an individual into the hypnodial state will provide you with a better understanding of what we mean.

EXAMPLE: "Make yourself as comfortable as you can and relax the best way you can. Just rest and relax while you listen to my voice. You do not need to concentrate on my voice. Just rest, relax and make yourself more comfortable. Move if you wish to do so to make yourself more and more comfortable. When you feel that you are completely relaxed and very comfortable, be still and let every nerve and muscle within your body relax. Let every bit of tension leave your body and mind. Just keep on resting, relaxing and loosen up every muscle in your arms and in your legs. Feel them become loose and limp as you keep on resting and relaxing more and more with each moment that passes. Soon you will feel your arms getting heavy, your legs will relax as they have never relaxed before. They too will become heavy. Every nerve and muscle within you is relaxing. Let yourself continue to relax and become loose and limp. Concentrate on something and let it appear as a mental picture within your mind. Anything that you can easily remember, that you have enjoyed very much, will help you to relax more and more. Just pay attention to that image within your mind which will soon appear. You have had wonderful times during your lifetime. Choose one of them and mentally bring it before your mind. Concentrate on it. Relax, relax, relax! Let all thoughts leave your mind. Do not allow anything to disturb you. Just relax, rest and enjoy that memory which is now coming before your mind. You will keep on resting. Nothing will bother you while you are resting and relaxing. Just letting every nerve, every muscle in your arms, your legs and in your body relax completely. Rest, rest, rest, relax, relax, RELAX!"

"You feel pleasantly warm and comfortable and are still just resting and relaxing. My voice guides you. Leads you into wonderful refreshing sleep. All sounds and noises are fading away. You will be unconcerned about any sound or noise outside of this room. Just relax. Let me lead you, direct you, so that you will feel wonderful on awakening from this soothing restful sleep which you are slowly going into. Do not resist in any way. Just relax. No harm will come to you. Nothing will happen. Do not wait for anything to happen. Just relax, rest and let yourself go into sleep. Just for a short while. Rest, relax and drift away into sleep. Your eyelids are heavy, heavy, heavy. They are so heavy. Too heavy to open. No matter how hard you try, your eyelids will not open. They are just too heavy. You cannot open your eyelids! You cannot, no matter how hard you try, you just cannot open your eyelids. They are heavy! Heavy! Heavy! Try, you cannot!"

This example of what a patter should convey to the mind of the person who is being hypnotized is just one of the many kinds hypnotists use. The more repetitious the suggestions are used, along with the monotonous tone and the inflection in the voice inferring that the suggestions are taking effect, the better the patter and the more successful will be the result. The method of induction is as important as the patter. Is the individual being hypnotized sitting or lying down? The patter must be in line with the condition of the person and in keeping with the position he is in. If he is sitting in a chair, it should mention that he is just getting drowsy and will just take a nap for a few moments. If he is lying down on a bed or couch, or seated in a reclining chair, he can be told that he will go into sleep. The thought of falling off of a chair may keep him from going into deep hypnosis. Everything should be taken into account. The welfare of the hypnotee is the uppermost thing to consider at all times. The hypnotee will feel your interest in his welfare and well being and go along with you more readily if you will bear in mind the thought that nothing matters to you except your responsibility to the person you are hypnotizing. Many times hypnotees will remark that they felt or sensed that you were protecting them in some way they couldn't explain. They picked up the feeling telepathically. They sensed they were in good hands and were willing to trust themselves in the care of the hypnotist. When this happens, you will find that your hypnotee can go into deep hypnosis more quickly and easily with each subsequent session.

Assuming that you are ready to work with your first hypnotee, let us go into a full patter and see how words can effect a person when formed into suggestions to induce a hypnotic condition. (The individual is lying down.)

PATTER

CLOSE YOUR EYES AND JUST RELAX. REST AND RELAX. REST, REST, REST! As you lie there quietly resting, make yourself more and more comfortable. In a few moments you will relax as you have never relaxed before. Do not be disturbed by my voice or any other sound or noise you may hear outside of this room. Just keep on resting and relaxing. Try to imagine that you are lying in bed in your own home. You are just resting and are going to take a short nap. For a while your mind will wander. Do not try to stop your thought or the pictures which may be going through your mind. Just relax, rest, rest and relax. In your mind will come the thought of sleep. My voice is a soothing voice. It calms your nerves, soothes the mind. Like a sedative taken to relax you, without interfering with your conscious mind, my voice will produce the same effect. It quiets the mind, allowing all thoughts to slowly fade away. All of your worries and cares of the day will slowly fade away and disappear entirely from your mind. Your conscious mind will become calm, quiet and still. You will begin to relax, rest and let every nerve and muscle within your body become loose and limp. You will feel so good, so relaxed. You will desire more and more of this wonderful, delightful feeling which is coming upon you. You are tired, tired, tired! Beginning to feel pleasantly warm and comfortable all over. From the top of your head down to the tips of your toes, you are relaxing. Relaxing more and more. Resting and relaxing. Quietly resting. Just relaxing. Very tired. Tired. Tired. Your eyelids are heavy! Very heavy. Too heavy to open. Do not try to open your eyes. Just rest and relax. Let nothing interfere with you. Do not allow anything to disturb you. Rest, rest, rest and relax. Relax all over. Let every nerve and muscle continue to relax. You are so very tired. Tired all over. Tired and drowsy. Your arms become heavy. The more you relax, the more tired and drowsy you feel. Just rest. Rest and relax. In a few moments all thoughts will leave your mind and you will feel so drowsy, you will desire to sleep. You will let yourself go into sleep. You will just drift away into sleep. A wonderful refreshing sleep. On awakening from this sleep you will feel and be physically fit and mentally alert, well able to handle everything that comes your way, efficiently, orderly and well. Just rest and relax and slowly let yourself go drifting, drifting, drifting down into sleep.

All thoughts are leaving your mind. You are very tired. Your arms are heavy, your legs are heavy, your body is relaxing. Every organ, every nerve and every muscle within your entire being is relaxing now. Relaxing as they have never relaxed before and it feels so good, so pleasant. It is a very soothing, delightful feeling. All thoughts are gone from your mind. You are still relaxing and quietly resting. Body and mind are resting. Just resting and relaxing. Your arms, your legs and your body continue to relax and you feel heavy. Heavy all over. Keep on relaxing, relax, relax! Body and mind just relaxing, resting, quietly resting. Tired and sleepy. Very tired, sleepy and drifting down into sleep. Let all thoughts leave your mind. Every bit of tension in body and mind is leaving. Going away, making you more and more sleepy. Go deep into sleep. Let yourself go as far as you can into a wonderful, restful sleep. All of your worries, cares and troubles of the day are gone from your mind. Just rest, relax and sleep. Go deep into sleep. Let yourself go deeper and deeper with each breath you take, relaxing as you have never relaxed before and enjoying every moment of this pleasant soothing sleep. Still aware of my voice. Always aware of my voice so that I may lead you, guide you and direct you, deeper and deeper down into sleep. When you will awaken, your entire body will remain relaxed. But, your mind will be very alert, clear, calm and sharp to everything that concerns you and you will be able to handle anything that comes your way very well. You will be able to think clearly and take care of anything that comes your way very efficiently, orderly and well. Your conscious mind will be alert to every opportunity which will come your way. You will have confidence in yourself, in your talk, in your walk and in your work. You will, on awakening, feel wonderful. You will have urges and desires to work and do things to better yourself. Each and every night you will sleep well. On retiring for the night, the moment your head hits the pillow, your whole entire being will relax and you will drift away into a deep, sound, refreshing sleep. Every nerve, muscle, organ, gland, fiber and ligament within your body will relax the moment you lie down to go to sleep. Your mind will be free of all tension, all worries and all cares. They will all disappear and you will drift away into a deep, sound sleep. Your body will rejuvinate and regenerate, your mind will become re-vitalized, so that on awakening you shall and you will awaken healthy and strong in body and mind. You will have a great urge and desire to better yourself in every way, physically and mentally. While you are asleep, nothing will bother or disturb you in any way. Nothing will upset you emotionally or in any manner whatsoever. You will awaken immediately in case of an emergency, with your mind alert, clear, calm and sharp and you will be well able to handle whatever it may be, in a calm, orderly and efficient manner. With confidence at all times, you shall and you will be able to cope with any condition, any situation, any opportunity which may arise. You will use confidence, you will have dynamic self confidence in your own ability to advance and better yourself. No matter where you may be, no matter what may confront you, at all times you will be keenly alert while you are awake, think clearly and be very well able to handle every-thing perfectly. You will be consciously aware of every-thing that concerns you. You shall and you will awaken each and every morning with your mind well rested and revitalized, your body relaxed and rejuvinated and every nerve and muscle, organ and gland within your body regenerated so that you will feel refreshed, alert to everything that concerns you and be full of vim, vigor and vitality, full of pep and energy, and with urges and desires to do things which will help you to advance in every way, physically and mentally. Continue to rest and keep on relaxing every nerve and muscle, every organ and gland within your body. You feel pleasantly warm and very comfortable. Sleep, sleep, sleep. In a few moments you will awaken feeling wonderful in every way from head to toes. I am going to count from one to ten, at the end of the count of ten, you will open your eyes and awaken, feeling completely rested, relaxed, refreshed and well able to take care of everything that concerns you. You shall and you will obey and comply with each and every suggestion now implanted within your mind. Let them become a part of your own way of thinking. Let them grow like seeds and become stronger within your mind so that you shall and you will be able to think in a positive way at all times from now on. Desiring to better yourself and your conditions, from now on, you will be positive in your thinking and in your actions and handle yourself with confidence, feeling secure at all times in the knowledge that you have confidence and control of your body and mind at all times from now on. On awakening, all of the heaviness, tiredness and sleep will be gone from your body and mind. You shall and you will feel and be perfectly normal and natural in every way, physically and mentally, healthy and strong in body and mind. I shall begin to count now and as I count from one to ten, you will slowly awaken. At the end of the count of ten, open your eyes and awaken, being normal and natural in every way. ONE . . . TWO . . . THREE . . . FOUR . . . FIVE . . . SLOWLY AWAKENING, ALL OF THE TIREDNESS, HEAVINESS AND SLEEP IS LEAVING YOUR BODY AND MIND. YOU ARE AWAKENING . . . SIX . . . SEVEN . . . EIGHT . . . YOU WILL HAVE COMPLETE CONTROL OF YOURSELF IN EVERY WAY ON AWAKENING . . . NINE . . . SLOWLY NOW, TAKE OVER COMPLETE CONTROL OF YOURSELF AND DO AS YOU PLEASE . . . TEN! OPEN YOUR EYES AND AWAKEN!"

This patter is a general patter which is used to relax a person and more or less initiate him into hypnosis. It has almost everything anyone would like to obtain. There is nothing in this patter to indicate that therapy is being applied. It consists of suggestions which have the ability to cause the subconscious to respond mentally without affecting the physical self. The next patter is made to include curative and therapeutic suggestions. Study them well.

It is hoped that you will realize how important it is to be careful of the words you use in hynosis. In formulating your patters always take into consideration the effect you desire to attain. Imagine that your words are as equal and as potent as medicine. Some hypnotees will respond well to any suggestions of physical well being. Some will need specific suggestions, directing the subconscious to certain parts of the body. In many cases, suggestions to the effect that they will respond to the kind of therapy they are receiving, will be sufficient. Whenever the desired results are not obtained in a few sessions, it is wise to reconsider and evaluate the words you are using in your sug-gestions. Many individuals may not like what you are saying and not tell you that they are disturbed by what you suggest. In our own practice, we always use the general patter in the first session to enable the person we are working with to know what kind of suggestions will be implanted in the mind if they are to be hypno-tized. If we have succeeded in hypnotizing the person at the first session, we definitely know that they are accepting what they hear and will continue on and apply the curative or therapeutic suggestions or what-ever kind the case may warrant. It may be to break a habit, instill confidence, natural childbirth, recall memory, implant new urges and desires to get well, advance, or to better one's existing conditions. But, whatever the case may be, it is very necessary and vitally important to formulate the patter in such a manner, so that it will be directive in obtaining the result you want to achieve.

Imagine that we have gone through the general patter and the hypnotee is responding fairly well. Instead of going on and awakening him, we shall continue to apply the suggestions necessary for his welfare. In the general patter we have words suggesting to the hypnotee that he will become tired, heavy, drowsy, sleepy, etc. These words formed into a patter, or any words that suggest rest, relax and those used to induce a con-dition of hypnosis are called hypnotic suggestions. They imply that hypnosis will take effect sooner or later. Words formulated into a patter that suggest the work will be done internally are valued as important therapeutically. Therefore are called curative or therapeutic suggestions.

The patters given at this time will contain curative, therapeutic and mental suggestions which produce effects when implanted in the mind during hypnosis. Toward the end of the general patter, instead of saying, "ON AWAKENING ALL OF THE TIREDNESS, ETC., WILL BE GONE FROM YOUR BODY AND MIND," we will go on with the suggestions we wish to implant in the mind and then continue to the awakening, picking it up at the point where we begin with the instructions to awaken.

TO CONTROL THE HABIT OF SMOKING . . . "As a cigarette smoker you are never at your best. The habit of smoking is a bad and harmful one. You desire to control this habit knowing that if you do so, you can better yourself physically and mentally. You know it is detrimental to your welfare and well being. It is harmful to health, mental ability and success. You know that inhaling the vile poisons of tobacco in the form of smoke is doing you harm. The smoke you inhale is brought into immediate contact with absorbing lung tissue and creates degenerative changes in the vital organs and nerve-centers in your body. Inhaling smoke degrades the brain cells so that you cannot think clearly nor express yourself in normal manner. Smoking destroys mentally and harms the body, disqualifying your abilities in home and business. You do not need cigarettes or smoke tobacco of any kind. You derive no pleasure whatsoever from it. It is harmful and keeps you from thinking in a calm and clear manner. You do not like it! You do not care for it any longer! You are beginning to hate smoking! You cannot stand the taste of tobacco or smoke! You would not deliberately inhale smoke from a burning fire because you know that it would harm you. Why then smoke and inhale the poison from a cigarette? You now know better and you understand that the smoke from a burning fire and that from a cigarette are equal in doing harm. You realize this now and have made up your mind that you are through with it. You hate smoking cigarettes or tobacco of any kind! You cannot stand it any more. You would prefer to have a strong and healthy body and mind, and a sweet, clean and healthy taste in your mouth to that which you have had before. The odor of tobacco or anyone else smoking will not bother you in any way. But, smoke in your mouth will make you feel sick to your stomach. You are done with smoking and all that it stands for, forever! The craving for smoking is killed by your own decree. You will not miss a cigarette or suffer any consequences from discontinuing smoking. You are free from the habit! You have complete control of this habit and shall not and will not allow anything or anyone to interfere with this control at any time. You are the master of yourself. No cigarette can ever be the master over you ever again. You are free! You shall not and will not smoke again. You will gain better health and more mental power from now on, and be physically fit and mentally strong because smoking will never again interfere with your welfare and well being. You are free from the habit. You will not smoke a cigarette or any kind of tobacco again. From this very moment you have complete control of the habit. You will become healthier and stronger with each day that passes from now on."

TO CONTROL INSOMNIA . . . "Make no effort of any kind to sleep. You will just relax and let your mind become still. There is nothing you can do to encourage the state of mind to sleep. It will become void of thoughts and accept the approach of sleep when it comes. Do not wonder what is going to happen. Do not be suspicious or distrustful. Do not desire that anything take place, nor watch to see what may occur. Do not seek to analyze what I am saying or that which is on your mind. Be as unconcerned as you can be and indifferent to everything around you. Have confidence in yourself and in the outcome of this treatment. Just relax. Rest and let your mind free to listen to my voice. No harm can possibly come to you when you are lost in sleep. You cannot be deceived or influenced against your better judgment. Just relax and let things happen. Abandon yourself to the pleasant feeling of sleep. Without reservation, reluctance or misgiving accept the pleasant feeling of drifting into sleep. Concentrate on the feeling, it is so pleasant, so nice and delightful. It calms your nerves and soothes your body. It makes you relax more and more with each breath you take. Your eyes are closed. The eyelids have shut off all light and color from the outside world. Your ears are closed to all sounds and noises. You hear only my voice leading you on to sleep. You know that when you awaken from this wonderful sleep you are drifting into now, you will feel wonderfully refreshed in body and mind. Your entire being will be well rested and you will automatically relax and drift away into sleep the moment your head hits the pillow. You will sleep well. On awakening in the morning you will feel wonderful in every way. Nothing will bother you or disturb you while you are asleep. All of your fears are gone and you know that you can sleep. Your body is responding to sleep. It is relaxing more and more, and you continue to drift down into sleep. You will let yourself go into sleep each and every time you desire to do so, quickly and easily, from now on."

"When the day is done and you are ready to retire for the night, every bit of tension within your body and mind will leave and you will relax every nerve and muscle in your body. You will think only of relaxing and resting and let your mind wander to the beautiful things you have experienced. You will think how nice and pleasant, how easy it is, to just rest and relax. You will relax completely and gently drift into sleep. Body and mind will relax. Your thoughts will be only on resting, on how good it is to just lie quietly and let sleep come upon you. There is no need to think of sleep. It will come as sure as the following day will come. It will embrace you and release every bit of tension within your body and mind. On waking from this refreshing sleep, you will desire to do the same thing each and every night. You will find it very easy to do so because no longer will you have thoughts of not being able to sleep. No longer will you need to worry about sleep. It will come to you in a normal and natural way. You will enjoy a good nights rest. You will sleep soundly and have pleasant dreams. Nothing will disturb you or interfere with you in any manner, shape or form. Yet, at all times your mind will immediately awaken if any emergency arises and you will be well able to handle the situation in an orderly manner. You will think clearly, remain calm and be free of tension. Whatever you do will be done efficiently. You will have confidence in your ability to sleep and sleep well. You will believe that you can, you shall and you will be able to drift away into sleep the moment your head hits the pillow. You can sleep! You know that you can sleep well! You shall and you will, from now on, surrender yourself to sleep the moment it enwraps you in its embrace. From now on you will desire more and more of this wonderful ability to sleep well. Each and every night, from now on, you will find it very easy to go deeply asleep and enjoy every moment of it, feeling its delightful and refreshing embrace as it rejuvinates and regenerates your body and revitalizes your mind. You shall and you will, from now on, let yourself go into sleep without interfering, in any way, each and every night so that on awakening each morning you will feel and be full of vim, vigor and vitality, well able to handle the days labor efficiently, orderly and well. With a clear mind, free from tension and no worries or cares to think of, you will have confidence and use it in your walk, your talk and in your actions. Because you shall and you will, from now on, be able to sleep and sleep well each and every night!"

TO CONTROL OBESITY, EXCESSIVE EATING AND OVERWEIGHT. "You are no longer satisfied with your habit of eating. You know and realize that you are not at your best when you eat excessively. You also realize that your intake of food is in excess of your outlay, and that your body cannot compensate for this condition. It does not burn up the food you eat, but lets it accumulate as fat. This interferes with your metabolism, as it does not generate heat and energy which helps to free your body of superfluous fat. The remedy lies in eating less and increasing muscular work. This remedy you will apply at once, in a combination of outdoor life, exercise, massage and by indulging more in your favorite hobby, sport or anything else which will help you rid your body of the excessive fat. You will no longer eat any of the foods which you know are harmful and detrimental to you. You will eat less of the starchy foods, sweets, pies, cake, candy, pastries, ice cream, pudding, chocolate or desserts, and you will no longer indulge in liquids having fats like cream. You will diminish the amount of foods and liquids taken, especially at meals. You will completely digest what food you do eat, approving and enjoying eating less, feeling better in every way. By eating less you will become more attractive. You will have confidence in yourself and feel secure in the knowledge that you are getting better and better in every respect, healthier and stronger in body and mind. Your actions will be without fear, because your heart and lungs will not be interfered with by the accumulations of fat which degenerates and retards the action of every organ within your body. You will lose weight without harmful effects. You will lose weight gradually and gain in its stead vim, vigor and vitality. The fats within your body will disintegrate and be absorbed and disappear completely. All of the excessive fats within your entire being will disappear. The fat will dissolve and disappear without any detrimental or harmful effects, because you will eat less, become more active and enjoy eating less, digesting the foods you eat with pleasure and knowing that you are eating just enough to keep you healthy and strong in body and mind and no more. A new habit of eating will be established which will be nutritive and well balanced from now on."

The patters mentioned are a part of the whole entire procedure of hypnosis. After relaxation and tension release is attained, no matter what the state of hypnosis may be, the therapeutic suggestions should be implanted in the mind. The hypnotic suggestions differ from the curative kind. It is to be remembered that one works externally on the conscious mind and the other internally on the subconscious mind.

What we are trying to make the reader understand is, that it is not hypnosis itself which is responsible for the many magnificent and wonderful things it performs. It is the power of suggestion, the power in a spoken word or thought, which, when accepted by either another person or yourself will produce the effect, whether it be negative or positive. The kind of suggestion used in hypnosis varies with the individuals needs. It is not the ability to hypnotize which is of the greatest importance, it is what you can do after you have a person hypnotized that really counts and is the most vital and important thing in the science of hypnosis. To give you a better idea of how important it is to know what to say to a person under hypnosis, we will provide a few more suggestions which are used for different purposes.

FOR THE CONTROL OF DIABETES . . . "If the

organs or glands are not functioning properly, they shall and will begin to function in a normal and natural manner. Your pancreas shall and will function normally and naturally, healthy and strong. It will provide the body with normal amounts of sugar and not manufacture sugar in excess of the quantity needed to keep you healthy and strong in body and mind. The craving for sweets will leave you and the carbohydrates you consume as food will be properly assimilated. Every bit of nervous tension will leave your body and mind. You will be, in every way, well able to control yourself and your desire for sweets so that you will become normal and natural, healthy and strong, in body and mind, etc."

FOR THE CONTROL OF ALCOHOLISM, EXCESSIVE DRINKING.

"You are done with alcohol once and forever. The appetite for it is now destroyed within you. You are no longer tempted by anyone or anything to drink any kind of alcoholic drink. You know it destroys mentality and your understanding of your moral responsibilities. Drinking also interferes with your obligations to self and family. It creates changes in your physical body, destroying health and mental ability. It is very harmful to your physical well being. It effects your vital organs, the blood, tissue and everything that is within you, damaging all of them. You will no longer desire any kind of alcoholic drink in lieu of food. You will desire more of nutritional food and depend on them for the units of energy you require to remain healthy and strong in body and mind. You shall and you will, from now on, refrain completely from indulging in alcoholic beverages. It will be impossible for you to take a drink made of alcohol or desire this kind of drink for any conceivable reason. You will not miss it! You do not need it! You realize now the importance of changing your desire for drinking to that of good fresh air, good food, exercise and sleep, etc. etc."

The suggestions you have read are only a small part of the actual pattern presented to the individual while he is under the influence of hypnosis. There are also suggestions for almost every kind of mental or physical disorder existing in our civilization. Suggestions for use in hypnotic treatment are as important as any medicine. They are a part of therapy and as such should be considered vital to the welfare of all. Learning how to formulate the most positive and proper suggestion to be used for specific purposes is as important as learning how to hypnotize.

CONCLUSION

There are basic principals and fundamentals as well as standards to follow as in all sciences. The most important principal is your responsibility to the person you are hypnotizing. He has placed himself in your care, trusting you to take care of him while he is under the influence of hypnosis. A code of ethics is a pledge to oneself, as a hypnotist, and an oath to others, that you will abide by the standards of the science. The following is the code of ethics the authors adhere to in their private practice.

CODE OF ETHICS

I hereby pledge to abide by the articles that are written into this code of ethics. By these articles I shall and will conduct myself in the presence of all men.

ARTICLE 1. I shall and will respect and esteem all men, regardless of race, creed or color, who strive to advance the science of hypnotism.

ARTICLE 2. I shall and will encourage research in all phases of hypnotism under proper scientific supervision.

ARTICLE 3. I shall and will practice hypnotism with deep regard for the welfare of the individual.

ARTICLE 4. I shall and will practice with morals and manners above reproach or censure.

ARTICLE 5. I shall and will avoid any practice which may discredit the science of hypnotism.

ARTICLE 6. I shall and will always maintain deep regard for the human mind and the physical, mental and spiritual welfare of all those seeking my guidance.

ARTICLE 7. I shall and will always hold confidential anything that may be said or done by the hypnotee while under hypnosis.

ARTICLE 8. I shall and will strive to expose and prevent all malpractice of hypnotism.

ARTICLE 9. I shall and will stay within the limits of my knowledge of hypnotism and never humiliate, embarrass or do anything that may harm a hypnotee or endanger his physical well being.

ARTICLE 10. I shall and will always abide by my

pledge to this code of ethics. Therefore, I will never treat or attempt to cure any illness of body or mind without the supervision of the medical profession.

There are two principal factors important to success in hypnotizing. The first is PRESTIGE, the respect the individual has for the hypnotist. The second is RAP-PORT, the line of communication established during the induction of hypnosis which allows the hypnotist to communicate directly with the subconscious mind of the hypnotee. To give you a better understanding of what rapport is, imagine that you are on the phone and you are talking to the operator. The operator stands for the conscious mind of the hypnotee. You have been having trouble getting your party and you are request-ing that she get your party for you. When the con-nection is made she tells you, "Here is your party, sir. You may go ahead," She then waits until she hears your voice talking to the person she has connected you with and then disconnects herself from that particular line. You are now conversing with the other party, which in this case under hypnosis, would be the sub-conscious of the hypnotee. The operator was the con-necting link between you and your party up to the point of actual contact with the other party. She is not a part of the conversation and does not interfere with what you are saying once the connection has been made. If the connection is strong and clear, we call it a firmer rapport. When a firm rapport is established and se-cured by testing for the depth of hypnosis, the desired results will generally be obtained. It is essential that rapport be established. Without it genuine hypnosis does not exist.

There are six fundamentals which are considered to be necessarily present to obtain a deep hypnotic effect. In accord with whatever fundamentals are present, so will be the depth of hypnosis. If two are present, there is light hypnosis. If four are present, there is medium hypnosis. If all six are present, it will be found to be deep hypnosis. The six fundamentals are:

1 . . . CONCENTRATION
2 . . . COOPERATION
3 . . . WILLINGNESS
4 . . . PERSEVERANCE
5 . . . BELIEF (IMAGINATION)
6 . . . FAITH (TRUST)

Some hypnotees will exhibit a few fundamentals. Very few individuals will show all six fundamentals are at work. Those who do are usually somnambules. Although we know that approximately 15% of the population are somnambules, we seldom are confronted with them. These are the natural somnambules. The hypnotic somnambules are usually individuals who have been taught and trained to respond quickly and easily to the influence of hypnosis. With diligent persistance and effort on the part of the hypnotist and the six fundamentals introduced to the hypnotee, artificial somnambulism can be induced.

All hypnotees are not uniform in responding and are not moved by the suggestions from the hypnotist. In the lighter states, the hypnotee can think, reason and is able to even discuss matters with the hypnotist. He can resist or reject any suggestion he does not agree with. It is necessary to know when to prove, to reason, convince, or when to imply, insinuate, gently persuade, emphatically affirm, or decide to endeavor to form a mental picture within the mind of the hypnotee. Moral strength, desire and the will to be helped are factors to be studied. It is the hypnotee with a strong will and vivid imagination who is responsible for the results and by no means whatsoever is the hypnotist able to guarantee any success. Success or failure depends on the hypnotee and how many of the six fundamentals are at work helping him to acquire the depth of hypnosis necessary to success. If he wills himself to be helped and knows how to use his imagination, hypnosis will be effectively applied. He must demonstrate belief and trust in his ability to gain from each session with hypnosis.

Concentration depends largely on our likes and dislikes, feelings and sensations, and on how much importance we attach to whatever it is we are concentrating our attention on. Time is important, but time cannot be considered when endeavoring to induce a deep hypnosis. The first session can be very decisive. If the hypnotee is concentrating on the patter, he will cooperate more if the suggestions are to his liking. If he begins to feel such things as heavy eyelids, arms or legs, he will be more willing to go along, waiting for other things to happen. His willingness will produce a hypnoidal condition. The desire to feel more causes perseverance to begin to appear at work. His imagination begins to work in the second state of hypnosis vividly enough for him to believe he has been hypnotized. It depends on the kind of faith and trust he has in the hypnotist and himself which determines the depth of hypnosis from then on. Prestige is working and the rapport has been established, but it is weak. If the hypnotee has explicit trust and presents confidence in his and the hypnotist's ability, he will follow where he is led and directed, strengthening the rapport and reaching into deep hypnosis. His mind and body, completely relaxed and free of tension, now are in tune with the hypnotist, both are as one. Rapport is the tuning of two or more minds into one channel. Once this link between the minds is established, possibilities become unlimited. It is not uncommon to see a hypnotee awaken out of hypnosis before he is told to do so. The cause is usually the loss of rapport or prestige.

In every science there are rules and regulations which govern a man's behavior, control conditions and safeguard all concerned. The dangers in hypnosis arise only when these rules are not followed. The authors, as directors of The Hypnotism Center of California, have compiled a list of rules which are a part of their instructions to their students learning how to hypnotize. It is as follows:

RULES AND REGULATIONS

1.   Countermand all suggestions which deal with conditions such as feeling tired, heavy, drowsy, etc., before ending a hypnotic session.

2.   Countermand all suggestions which produce cataleptic conditions of rigidity before ending a session.

3.   Before the awakening countermand all suggestions of amnesia, hallucinations and anesthesia which have been produced during hypnosis for the purpose of testing.

4.   Countermand post-hypnotics which have been performed during the period of hypnosis which have been used to demonstrate hypnosis at work.

5.   Ascertain the condition of the person you hypnotized after the awakening and be sure that no after effects ensue on leaving your presence.

6.   Do not take things for granted and think that your hypnotee is normal after the session is over. Be sure that body and mind are normal, by questioning, in regards to feelings and sensations.

7.   Understand the effects of positive and negative suggestions.

8.   Study the operation of the minds. Familiarize yourself with all phases of mental health.

9.   Adapt yourself in such a manner so that your appearance, face or dress will not antagonize or distract the hypnotee.

10.   Let your actions and bearing be positive at all times.

11.   Never hesitate in words or action. Hesitation will often have a tendency to cause the hypnotee to de-hypnotize himself.

12.   Be competent in forming and making constructive suggestions.

13.   Establish confidence by remaining calm, work in a well balanced and masterful manner at all times.

14.   Never experiment with hypnotees. All experimentation should be done under the strict supervision of superiors and before qualified witnesses.

15.   When working with the opposite sex, always have a witness present.

16.   Leave all therapeutics to those who are qualified.

17.   Never attempt to hypnotize anyone without their permission.

18.   Read, study and attend lectures about hypnosis and any other subject matter dealing with the power of the mind.

19.   Stay within the limits of your own knowledge.

20.   Always remember your responsibility to the hypnotee.

21.   Remember at all times, that the hypnotee can sense things stronger in hypnosis than when he is wide awake. Never think of time or hasten to the awakening while you are working with hypnosis. The hypnotee may sense it and become irritable. You will lose prestige and weaken the rapport.

22.   Maintain a positive manner of speaking at all times and know exactly how long your patter will be and make sure that you can wind up the session at the time allotted

23.   Be sure to include suggestions of well-being,

physical fitness and mental alertness in your patter before you awaken the hypnotee.

24.   Remember that repetition does the work. All suggestions dealing with therapy or curative effects should be often repeated before, during and after hypnosis.

25.   Remember at all times to repeat your post-hypnotics before the awakening. It should always be the last words the hypnotee hears before he becomes consciously aware and wide awake. Example: "On awakening, you shall and you will obey and comply with the suggestions I have given you. You will, whenever I touch your right shoulder, immediately close your eyes and go into a deep, sound hypnotic sleep. Open your eyes and wake up!"

FACTS ON HYPNOSIS

It is one of the oldest sciences known to man, considering the fact that it has been used for thousands of years in all civilizations, yet, it is still the least known of all the sciences.

At the present time, it is being scientifically investigated.

In therapeutic fields it has no equal as an aid and ally to the sciences involved in mental and physical health. It is most useful in anodyne treatment.

It has no limits, no boundaries or language barriers. The fields of religion, medicine, education, sports, etc., have been opened and its powers are being explored.

Hypnosis has been known under many names, such as mesmerism, magnetism, electrical psychology, artificial somnambulism and animal magnetism.

The average person seeking help through hypnosis will usually ask these questions:
WHAT CAN HYPNOSIS DO FOR ME? Through hypnotic suggestions you can control habits, gain confidence, alleviate pain, release physical and mental tension, relax quickly and easily, improve memory and concentration, increase your ability and develop latent talents.
WILL I BE UNCONSCIOUS? No! Suggestions are implanted within the mind in the lighter stages of hypnosis. You will be aware of everything unless it is necessary to produce amnesia, analgesia and anesthesia

for major surgery or to obtain information through regression.

WILL THE RESULTS BE PERMANENT? Yes! But it is up to you. If you have a strong desire to make it permanent, and are willing and cooperative to accept and believe that it is your way of thinking and not the hypnotist who is merely talking to you, it will become a permanent part of your belief. Believing it will be, so it shall be!

DO I NEED A DOCTOR TO WORK WITH HYP-NOSIS? If you are under a doctor's care, he should be the one to advise hypnotherapy and refer you to a medical or professional hypnotist specializing in hypnotherapy. In cases where hypnotherapy is not applicable, there is no need for medical supervision.

WHY SHOULD I TRY HYPNOSIS? Everyone needs improving in some way, no matter who they are. Can you carry a positive attitude and act with poise under any circumstance, remain calm and think clearly at all times? Do you do your work well, efficiently and in an orderly manner? THINK! You will find many things in your life or in your existing conditions which you are not satisfied with. Hypnosis may help you to better yourself and your conditions.

The list of mental, physical and organic problems and ailments which have been treated successfully through hypnotic suggestions to date, is very large. Numerous types of fears, phobias, complexes, ailments and diseases are mentioned. A list will be sent on request. Address your letter to: THE HYPNOTISM CENTER OF CALIFORNIA, 8583 West Pico Blvd., Los Angeles,

California 90035, or send your request direct to the publisher.

To those before us who have delved deeply into the science of hypnosis, who have given us so much to go on, and to those who champion the cause and who have made hypnotism what it is today, we give our thanks and credit for all they have done. We sincerely desire that you and others of our time, interested in hypnosis, will continue to help to advance this wonderful science by using the information contained herein for the benefit and welfare of your fellow man.

ABOUT THE AUTHORS

ALBERTO HIDALGO, M.D. has been engaged in the practice of general surgery in Los Angeles since 1958. He is a member of The American Medical Association, California Medical Association, Los Angeles County Medical Association, American Society of Clinical Hypnosis and medical consultant of The Hypnotism Center of California, engaged in directing all phases of hypnotherapy.

JACK I. GRAY, Psychologist has been specializing in the practice of hypnosis for over 15 years. He is nationally known as the owner of The Hypno-Aid Company and director of the Hypnotism Center of California, both established in 1951. As a manufacturer and distributor of hypno-aids, he caters to the hypnotic profession throughout the world. Some of the machines that hypnotize are of his own invention. Since 1951 he has been recognized as an authority in his fields. Articles have been written about him and his hypno-aids in national magazines. As director of The Hypnotism Center of California, a school of instruction, he has taught doctors, dentists, and many others how to hypnotize. He has also taught many individuals the art of self hypnosis. He is a well known lecturer and demonstrator of hypnosis and self hypnosis. He is technical advisor and one of the directors of The California Association for Ethical Hypnosis.